COLLECTED ESSAYS
OF
EDMUND GOSSE

VOL. III

CRITICAL KIT-KATS

BY THE SAME AUTHOR
Uniform with this Volume

SEVENTEENTH-CENTURY STUDIES
GOSSIP IN A LIBRARY
FRENCH PROFILES
PORTRAITS AND SKETCHES

NEW YORK
CHARLES SCRIBNER'S SONS

CRITICAL KIT-KATS

BY

EDMUND GOSSE, C.B.

NEW YORK

CHARLES SCRIBNER'S SONS

1914

Printed in England

Dedication

To THOMAS HARDY

My Dear Hardy,

You will recollect, I think—for we have often laughed over the little incident—how, many years ago, you and I, having lost our way in the leafy mazes of the borough of Bridport, asked a grave young man our road to the railway-station. Not content with misdirecting us, the scoundrel must needs officiously conduct us up terraced paths, and between walls clustered with creepers, until he had seen us fairly started on the highway that led out of the opposite end of the town. How angry we were when we found out that we had been duped, and how astonished! I asked you, bitterly, if this was the vaunted courtesy of your Wessex yokel. As we kicked our heels at last, much too late for the train, in the blank waiting-room, we speculated on the psychology of the thing. Was Bridport, above all other towns, the abode of inhospitable crime, or was the young man an outlaw, flying from justice, and glad to revenge himself on the very prophet of his county? Or, was it not rather to be believed, as your kind heart, grown philosophical, suggested, that the young man, shocking as his advice had proved, gave it in good faith, knowing no better?

At all events, we two go no more to Bridport. Perhaps, as your people say, "Bridport is Bridport still." It remains with us, at least, as a symbol for misleading criticism, and that dark young man as the very Zoilus of his parish. In sending you another book of mine—such a poor return, at best, for your beautiful sylvan stories—how can I but wonder whether my sign-board work may not after all be of the Bridport order? What if every judgment in it but misleads and misdirects? A terrible nightmare, under which my only consolation is that you, even if you find me a false guide, will extend to me the indulgence which finally determined that our solemn miscreant, that hot summer afternoon, could not have meant to deceive, but only "knew no better."

Take the little book, then, for the sake of the comrade, not of the critic. Take it as a landmark in that friendship, to me inestimably precious, which has now lasted more than twenty years, and will continue, I hope and think, unbroken till one or other of us can enter into no further earthly relations.

I am always, my dear Hardy,

Yours sincerely,

E. G.

PREFACE

In an age when studies multiply, and our shelves groan with books, it is not every interesting and original figure to whom the space of a full-length or even a half-length portrait can be spared. For the low comfortable rooms where people dined in the last century, there was invented the shorter and still less obtrusive picture called a Kit-Kat,* and some of our most skilful painters have delighted in this modest form of portraiture, which emphasises the head, yet does not quite exclude the hand of the sitter. I have ventured to borrow from the graphic art this title for my little volume, since these are condensed portraits, each less than half-length, and each accommodated to suit limited leisure and a crowded space.

They are essays in a class of literature which it is strange to find somewhat neglected in this country, since, if it can only be executed with tolerable skill, none should be more directly interesting and pleasing. We are familiar with pure criticism and with pure biography, but what I have here tried to produce is a combination

* Or a Kit-Cat, for both forms are in use.

of the two, the life illustrated by the work, the work relieved by the life. Such criticism as is here attempted is not of the polemical order; the biography excludes that. We cease to be savage and caustic when we are acquainted with the inner existence of a man, for the relentlessness of satire is only possible to those who neither sympathise nor comprehend. What is here essayed is of the analytical, comparative, and descriptive order; it hopes to add something to historical knowledge and something to æsthetic appreciation. It aims, in short, at presenting a little gallery of contemporary kit-kats, modest in proportion, but large enough to show the head and the hand.

Of the genesis of these essays, it may be sufficient to say that several of them originated in the fact that I was able to add something to the positive knowledge of a figure suddenly made the object of increased curiosity. In several cases, I have been aided by the family of the subject, or by persons in possession of facts not hitherto made public. In particular, in two instances, that eminent poet who for many years honoured me with his friendship, Robert Browning, laid upon me as a duty the publication of what I have written. What is here found, in matters of fact, regarding the Sonnets of his Wife and the incidents of the career of Beddoes, comes with the authority and is presented at the desire of

Browning. I need not produce my credentials in each case, but I may be allowed to say that there is only one of these essays in which I have been able to add nothing, either from the report of others or from my own observation, to biographical knowledge. In several, the personal impression is almost entirely my own or contributed to me from unprinted sources.

If it should be suggested that these little studies leave much unsaid and are far from exhausting the qualities of their subjects, I can but put myself, while admitting the charge to the full, under the protection of the most genial of all great men of letters, and borrow what Lafontaine says in the immortal epilogue to the *Contes:*

> Bornons ici cette carrière :
> Les longs ouvrages me font peur ;
> Loin d'épuiser une matière,
> On n'en doit prendre que la fleur.

That I have secured the fine flower of any of these delicate spirits is more than I dare hope, but to do so has at least been my aim and my design.

LONDON, *February* 1896.

CONTENTS

	Page
The Sonnets from the Portuguese	1
Keats in 1894	19
Thomas Lovell Beddoes	29
Edward FitzGerald	63
Walt Whitman	93
Count Lyof Tolstoï	113
Christina Rossetti	133
Lord De Tabley	163
Toru Dutt	197
M. José-Maria de Heredia	213
Walter Pater	239
Robert Louis Stevenson	273

Of the following Essays, those on "The Sonnets from the Portuguese" and "Thomas Lovell Beddoes" were originally printed as prefaces to editions of the poems, issued by Mr. J. M. Dent. For his kind permission to reprint them my thanks are due to him, as for similar courtesy to the proprietors of "The Fortnightly Review," "The Contemporary Review," "The New Review," and "The Century Magazine." All the Essays have been carefully revised, and in several cases considerably enlarged.

THE SONNETS
FROM THE PORTUGUESE

The Sonnets from the Portuguese

IT was in the second or 1850 edition of the *Poems in two volumes* that the *Sonnets from the Portuguese* were first given to the public. The circumstances attending their composition have never been clearly related. Mr. Browning, however, eight years before his death, made a statement to a friend, with the understanding that at some future date, after his own decease, the story might be more widely told. The time seems to have arrived when there can be no possible indiscretion in recording a very pretty episode of literary history.

During the months of their brief courtship, closing, as all the world knows, in the clandestine flight and romantic wedding of September 12, 1846, neither poet showed any verses to the other. Mr. Browning, in particular, had not the smallest notion that the circumstances of their betrothal had led Miss Barrett into any artistic expression of feeling. As little did he suspect it during their honeymoon in Paris, or during their first crowded weeks in Italy. They settled, at length, in Pisa; and being quitted by Mrs. Jamieson and her niece, in a very calm and happy mood the young couple took up each his or her separate literary work.

Their custom was, Mr. Browning said, to write alone, and not to show each other what they had written. This was a rule which he sometimes broke through, but she never. He had the habit of working in a downstairs room, where their meals were spread, while Mrs. Browning studied in a room on the floor above. One day, early in 1847, their breakfast being over, Mrs. Browning went upstairs, while her husband stood at the window watching the street till the table should be cleared. He was presently aware of some one behind him, although the servant was gone. It was Mrs. Browning, who held him by the shoulder to prevent his turning to look at her, and at the same time pushed a packet of papers into the pocket of his coat. She told him to read that, and to tear it up if he did not like it; and then she fled again to her own room.

Mr. Browning seated himself at the table, and unfolded the parcel. It contained the series of sonnets which have now become so illustrious. As he read, his emotion and delight may be conceived. Before he had finished it was impossible for him to restrain himself, and, regardless of his promise, he rushed upstairs, and stormed that guarded citadel. He was early conscious that these were treasures not to be kept from the world; "I dared not reserve to myself," he said, "the finest sonnets written in any language since Shakespeare's." But Mrs. Browning was very loth indeed to consent to the publication of what had been the very notes and chronicle of her betrothal. At length she was persuaded to permit her friend, Miss Mary Russell Mitford, to whom they had originally been sent in manuscript, to pass them through the press, although she absolutely declined to accede to Miss Mitford's suggestion that they should appear in one of the fashionable annuals of the day. Accordingly a small volume was printed entitled *Sonnets | by | E. B. B. | Reading | Not for Publication | 1847 |* , an octavo of 47 pages.

When it was determined to publish the sonnets in the volumes of 1850, the question of a title arose. The name which was ultimately chosen, *Sonnets from the Portuguese*, was invented by Mr. Browning, as an ingenious device to veil the true authorship, and yet to suggest kinship with that beautiful lyric, called *Catarina to Camoens*, in which so similar a passion had been expressed. Long before he ever heard of these poems, Mr. Browning called his wife his "own little Portuguese," and so, when she proposed "Sonnets translated from the Bosnian," he, catching at the happy thought of "translated," replied, "No, not Bosnian—that means nothing—but from the Portuguese! They are Catarina's sonnets!" And so, in half a joke, half a conceit, the famous title was invented.

I

The psychological moment at which the *Sonnets from the Portuguese* were composed, was one of singular importance. Although she was in her forty-first year (according to some accounts, in her thirty-eighth), the genius of Elizabeth Barrett was but newly come to its maturity. In precocity of intelligence she had been so remarkable as to become a type of childish attainment, but as an artist she was very slow to develop. Her earliest writings were strictly imitative; the volumes she published in her young womanhood were full of interesting passages, but crude and jejune to an extraordinary degree. Had Elizabeth Barrett died at the age of thirty-three,* that is to say immediately after the publication of *The Seraphim*, she would scarcely live among the English poets. It is to a subsequent period, it is to the years between the loss of her brother Edward at Torquay and her marriage, that those poems belong which display her talent at their highest achievment. The two volumes of 1844 lifted her by a bound to the highest place among the living poets of her country, and seated her by the side of Tennyson. These two, in the genial old age of Wordsworth, were left the sole obvious inheritors of his throne, for Robert Browning was still obscure save to a very few.

The change that in those years preceding her betrothal had come to Elizabeth Barrett was a purifying and crystallising one. She had always had fire, and she was to keep the coal burning on her tongue, like the prophet, until the end of her career. But in the early period, and again in the period of her decline, what

---

* I take for granted that the Coxhoe date of her birth, March 6, 1806, must be the correct one. But the crux seems still unsettled.

was lacking was light. Her style was turbid; the poet was not Sappho, standing in sunlight on the cliff of Mitylene, but Pythia, seated in the smoke and vapour of Delphi, tortured by the vehemence of her own utterance, torn by the message which she lacked the art to deliver. Critics are beginning to see now, and sorrowfully to admit, that what is causing the noble figure of Elizabeth Barrett to recede gradually from that front place in which Tennyson, for instance, and Keats hold their pre-eminence, is her turbidity. The best poetry may roll down violent places, but it remains as limpid as a trout-stream; what is unfortunate about Mrs. Browning's is that it is constantly stained and clouded.

But there was a period—we may roughly date it between 1842 and 1850—when these radical faults affected her style least. It was then that she reached the zenith of her genius, and, by a strange and fortunate accident, it was then, also, that she attained her greatest sum of happiness and health. Of this highest period, the summit or peak was the short space during which Robert Browning visited her as her affianced lover, and it is not singular, perhaps, but it is at least very interesting and pleasing, to find her writings at that moment less affected than at any other time, before or afterwards, by the errors which beset her.

In other words, the *Sonnets from the Portuguese*, although they are by no means of equal merit, reach at their best the highest art of which their author was capable, and if we did not possess them, we should be forced to form a considerably lower estimate of her possibilities as an artist than we now do. She seems in the very best of her work, outside the volumes of 1844, to be utterly indifferent to technical excellence. Even in those volumes we see that her laxity was absolutely inherent, and that she is always liable to imperfection and licence. But the *Sonnets from the Portuguese* prove that she could, at her purest, throw off these stains and blemishes, and cast her work in bronze, like a master. They show her to us at her very best, and they form the pinnacle of her edifice as an artistic constructor. Perhaps, and to some readers, they may be neither the most attractive nor the most amusing of her writings, but to the critic they are certainly the least imperfect.

II

The natural bent of Elizabeth Barrett was certainly not to the sonnet. She was too dithyrambic, too tumultuous, to be willingly restrained within a rigid form of verse. She employed none other of the regular English metres, except blank verse, which she treated with a sort of defiant desperation, and *terza rima*, in which she successfully strangled her genius. Her lyrics are all of her own invention or adaptation, and they are commonly of a loose, wild form, fit to receive her chains of adverbial caprices and her tempestuous assonances. But her love of Shakespeare and Wordsworth drove her to emulation, and once and again she strove to bind her ebullient melodies down to the strict mould of fourteen rhymed iambics. It is evident that the difficulties she encountered piqued her to return to the attack, for her occasional sonnets became more and more frequent. It is interesting to note that, as befitted so learned a student of the Italians, her sonnets, from the first, were accurately built on the Petrarchan model. We might have expected from her usual laxity of form an adherence to the Elizabethan quatorzain, or, at least, to some of those adaptations in which Wordsworth, Coleridge, and even Keats indulged. But Miss Barrett, throughout her career, was one of the most rigid of Petrarchans, and no fault can be found with the structure of her octetts and sestetts.

One of the earliest sonnets of her mature period was that entitled "The Soul's Expression," which is so interesting as a revelation of her own consciousness of the difficulties which technical art presented to her, and so valuable an indication of the mode in which she approached the sonnet-form, that it may here be quoted :—

> *With stammering lips and insufficient sound,*
> *I strive and struggle to deliver right*
> *That music of my nature, day and night*
> *With dream and thought and feeling, interwound,*
> *And inly answering all the senses round*
> *With octaves of a mystic depth and height,*
> *Which step out grandly to the infinite*
> *From the dark edges of the sensual ground!*
> *This song of soul I struggle to outbear*
> *Through portals of the sense, sublime and whole,*

*And utter all myself into the air:
But if I did it—as the thunder-roll
Breaks its own cloud—my flesh would perish there,
Before that dread apocalypse of soul.*

Fine as this is, eminently true to her own mood, and singular for its self-knowledge, it cannot be said to promise for its writer any great felicity as a sonneteer. The perturbed imagery, the wild grammar, the lack of a clarified and disciplined conception of style are prominent in every line. Very much more successful, however, and plainly inspired by the study of Wordsworth, is the famous sonnet, "On a Portrait by R. B. Haydon," and in the years that immediately followed her return from Torquay, Miss Barrett's sonnets came thicker and faster, with a steady increase in the power to give her own peculiar characteristics of expression to this unfamiliar instrument. But the *Sonnets from the Portuguese* went further still. The little harp or lyre she had laboriously taught herself to perform upon, had just become familiar to her fingers, when it was called upon to record emotions the most keen, and imaginations the most subtle, which had ever crossed the creative brain of its possessor.

Great technical beauty, therefore, is the mark of these wonderful poems. Not merely are the rhymes arranged with a rare science and with a precision which few other English poets have had the patience to preserve, but the tiresome faults of Miss Barrett's prosody, those little foxes which habitually spoil her grapes, are here marvellously absent. Her very ear, which sometimes seemed so dull, with its "morning" and "inurning," its "Bacchantes" and "grant us," here seems to be quickened and strung into acuteness. There is a marked absence, in the *Sonnets from the Portuguese*, of all slovenly false rhymes, of all careless half-meaningless locutions, of all practical jokes played upon the parts of speech. The cycle opens with a noble dignity, and it is, on the whole, preserved at that high ethical level of distinguished poetic utterance.

Of sonnet-cycles in the English language, there are but very few which can even be mentioned in connection with that which we are describing. In the Elizabethan age, many crowns woven of fourteen-petalled blossoms were laid at the feet of unknown ladies. The art which invested these groups of sonnets was mainly of a thin and conventional order. It would task the memory or the instinct of the best of English scholars to tell at sight whether a given sonnet came from the garland of *Idea* or of *Fidessa*, of *Delia* or of *Chloris*. Two cycles in that age immensely surpassed all the rest, and we may safely say that the *Amoretti* of Spenser form a set of poems as much greater than those we have mentioned, as they are inferior to Shakespeare's. In later times, we have one or two deliberate sets of sonnets by Wordsworth, and since the days of Mrs. Browning, Rossetti's *House of Life*. In foreign poetry, it is natural to turn to the *Sonettenkranz*, in which, in 1807, Goethe darkly celebrated his passion for Minna Herzlieb, the mysterious Ottilie of the

Wahlverwandtschaften. Among the five best or most striking prolonged poems in the sonnet-form which English literature possesses, Miss Barrett's, however, must unquestionably be reckoned. No competent critic could put the languid sweetness and honeyed vagueness of Spenser's daisy-chain of quatorzains in a rank so high as these serried, nervous, and highly-developed poems must hold, while Wordsworth, perfect as he constantly is in the evolution of a single sonnet, is scarcely to be applauded for his conduct of any such series of such poems, nor *The River Duddon* or *The Ecclesiastical Sonnets* to be compared for vital interest with those we are considering. Miss Barrett, accordingly, is left, on this occasion, with but two competitors. Rossetti excels her by the volume and impetus of his imagery, and by his voluptuous intrepidity, but she holds her own by the intense vivacity of her instinct and the sincerity of her picture of emotion. Beside the immortal melodies of Shakespeare, hers may be counted voluble, harsh, and slight; but even here, her sympathy with a universal passion, the freshness and poignancy with which she treats a mood that is not rare and almost sickly, not foreign to the common experience of mankind, but eminently normal, direct, and obvious, give her a curious advantage. It is probable that the sonnets written by Shakespeare to his friend contain lovelier poetry and a style more perennially admirable, but those addressed by Elizabeth Barrett to her lover are hardly less exquisite to any of us, and to many of us are more wholesome and more intelligible.

III

Sincerity, indeed, is the first gift in literature, and perhaps the most uncommon. It is not granted to more than a few to express in precise and direct language their most powerful emotional experiences. To those who, like Mary Magdalene, have loved much, the art is rarely given to define and differentiate their feelings. The attempt to render passion by artistic speech is commonly void of success to a pathetic degree. Those who have desired, enjoyed, and suffered to the very edge of human capacity, put the musical instrument to their lips to try and tell us what they felt, and the result is all discord and falsetto. There is no question that many of the coldest and most affected verses, such as we are apt to scorn for their tasteless weakness, must hide underneath the white ash of their linguistic poverty a core of red hot passion. But the rare art of literary sincerity has not been granted to these inarticulate lovers, and what cost them so many tears affords us nothing but fatigue or ridicule.

It is peculiarly true that women who are poets can or will but seldom take us truly into their confidence in this matter. A natural but unfortunate delicacy leads them to write of love so platonically or so obscurely that we cannot tell what it is they wish to communicate. Not to seem so unmaidenly as to address a man, they feign to be men themselves and languish at the ladies. We are as much interested and as much convinced as we are at the opera when broad-hipped cavaliers in silken tights dance with slightly shorter girls in skirts. It is a curious fact that the amount of love-poetry written by women, and openly addressed to men, is very scanty. Our poetesses write:

> *I made a posy for my Love*
> *As fair as she is soft and fine,*

and wonder that we are faintly interested. It should be " as tough as he is firm and strong," and then we might really be inclined to conclude that the ditty was inspired by experience or instinctive feeling. Lady Winchelsea's honest praises of her husband, Ephelia's couplets on that false J. G. who sailed away to Tangier and never came back again, the sonnets of the fair rope-maker of Lyons, Louise Labé, the tender, thrilling lyrics written three hundred years later by Marceline Desbordes-Valmore—these are almost the only poems in all literature which one remembers as dealing, in lucidity and sincerity alike, with the love of a man by a woman.

But the keynote of Elizabeth Barrett as an artist was sincerity. It is this quality, with all that it implies, which holds together the edifice of her style, built of such incongruous materials that no less-tempered mortar could bind it into a compact whole. At no period of her literary life, even when she was too slavishly following obsolete or tasteless models, was she otherwise than sincere. She was not striving to produce an effect; she was trying with all the effort of which her spirit was capable, to say exactly what was in her heart. When sorrow possessed her, her verse sobbed and wailed with impatient human stress, and when at last, while she waited for Death to take her by the hair, it was Love instead who came, she poured forth the heart of a happy woman without stint or concealment. The typical instance of the former class is the poem called "De Profundis," written as soon after the drowning of her brother Edward as the shattered nerves and beaten brain permitted her to taste the solace of composition. It should be read, in spite of its comparative inferiority, in connection with the *Sonnets from the Portuguese*, for the power it reveals is the same; it is the capacity, while feeling acutely and deeply, to find appropriate, sufficient, and yet unexaggerated expression for the emotion. This great neuropathic artist was a physician as well as a sufferer, and could count her pulses accurately through all the spasms of her anguish and her ecstasy.

When, in 1866, Robert Browning published the first selection from his wife's poems, he arranged the pieces in such a way as to give unobtrusive emphasis to the connection between the *Sonnets from the Portuguese* and two short lyrics. Even if he had not placed "Question and Answer," and "Inclusions" immediately in front of the sonnet-cycle, we might have been justified in conjecturing that they belonged to the same period and the same mood. The arrangement of the *Sonnets* is historical. They are not heaped together in accidental sequence, as Spenser's and Shakespeare's seem to be, but they move on from the first surprise of unexpected passion to the final complete resignation of soul and body in a rapture which is to be sanctified and heightened by death itself. It is therefore possible, I think, by careful examination of the text, to insert in the sequence of sonnets, at their obvious point of composition, the two lyrics I have just mentioned; and for that purpose I will quote them here.

Taking the *Sonnets* in our hands, we meet first with the record of the violent shock produced on the whole being of the solitary and fading recluse by the discovery that Love—laughing Love masquerading under the cowl of Death—has invaded her sequestered chamber. Then to amazement succeeds instinctive repulsion; she shrinks back in a sort of horror, in her chilly twilight, from the boisterous entrance of so much heat and glow. But this quickly passes, also, submerged in the sense of her own unworthiness; her hands are numb, her eyes blinded and dazed—what has this guest of kings to do with her, a mourner in the dust? Then follows, in a crescent movement of emotion, the noble image of Electra, pouring her sepulchral urn and all its ashes at the feet of Love, ashes that blight and burn, an affection so morbid and vain that it may rather destroy than bless the heart which provokes the gift. It is at this moment, I think, between sonnets 5 and 6, that "Question and Answer" should be read, repeating the same idea, but repeating it in a lower key, with less violence and perhaps a shade less conviction:

> *Love you seek for, presupposes*
> *Summer heat and sunny glow.*
> *Tell me, do you find moss-roses*
> *Budding, blooming in the snow?*

Snow might kill the rose-tree's root—
Shake it quickly from your foot,
   Lest it harm you as you go.

From the ivy where it dapples
   A grey ruin, stone by stone,
Do you look for grapes or apples,
   Or for sad green leaves alone?
Pluck the leaves off, two or three—
Keep them for morality
   When you shall be safe and gone.

But above these flutterings of the captured heart the captor hangs enamoured and persistent, smiling at the fiat which bids him begone: and the heart begins to thaw with the unrelieved radiation. The poetess acknowledges that she feels that she will stand henceforward in his shadow, that he has changed for her the face of all the world. Still, she dares not yield. The tide of her unworthiness flows up, and floods all the creeks of her being; she can but hide her eyes, from which the tears are flowing, and bid him, if he will not go and leave her, if he will persist in standing there with eloquent eyes fixed upon her, to trample on the pale stuff of her life, too dead to be taken to his arms. She is scarcely reasonable; we feel her pulses reeling, her limbs failing, and in the next sonnet the wave recedes for the final forward rush. She will not pour her poison on to his Venice-glass, she will not love him, will not see him—and in the next line she is folded to his arms, murmuring, "I love thee . . . I love thee!"

From this point forward the sonnets play, in their exquisite masque, as if to celestial dance-music, with the wild thoughts and tremulous frolics of accepted love, with a pulse that ever sinks into more and more normal beat, with an ever steadier and deeper flush of the new-born life. And here, if the reader will lay down the book at the close of sonnet 18, he may interpolate the lovely lyric called "Inclusions":

Oh, wilt thou have my hand, Dear, to lie along in thine?
As a little stone in a running stream, it seems to lie and pine.
Now drop the poor pale hand, Dear, unfit to pledge with thine.

Oh, wilt thou have my cheek, Dear, drawn closer to thine own?
My cheek is white, my cheek is worn, by many a tear run down.
Now leave a little space, Dear, lest it should wet thine own.

Oh, must thou have my soul, Dear, commingled with thy soul?
Red grows the cheek, and warm the hand; the part is in the whole:
Nor hands nor cheeks keep separate, when soul is joined to soul.

We may pursue no further, save in the divine words of the sonnets themselves, the record of this noble and exquisite "marriage of true minds." But we may be thankful that the accredited chronicle of this episode in life and literature, lifted far out of any vagueness of conjecture or possibility of misconstruction, exists for us, distinguishing, illuminating, perfuming a great page of our national poetry. Many of the thoughts that enrich mankind and many of the purest flowers of the imagination had their roots, if the secrets of experience were made known, in actions, in desires, which could not bear the light of day, in hot-beds smelling quite otherwise than of violet or sweetbriar. But this cycle of admirable sonnets, one of the acknowledged glories of our literature, is built patently and unquestionably on the union in stainless harmony of two of the most distinguished spirits which our century has produced.

KEATS IN 1894

Keats in 1894

Address delivered at Hampstead on occasion of the unveiling of the American Monument, July 16, 1894.

IT is with no small emotion that we receive to-day, from the hands of his American admirers, a monument inscribed to the memory of Keats. Those of us who may be best acquainted with the history of the poet will not be surprised that you have convened us to the church of Hampstead, although it was not here that he was born, nor here that he died. Yet some who are present to-day may desire to be reminded why it is that when we think of Keats we think of Hampstead. It is in his twenty-first year, in 1816, that we find the first record of his ascent of this historic eminence. He appears, then, on the brow of Hampstead Hill as the visitor, as the disciple, of Leigh Hunt, in his cottage in the Vale-of-Health, a cottage, so I am told, to this day the haunt of poets. He comes, an ardent lad, with great, flashing eyes, and heavy, golden curls, carrying in his hand a wreath of ivy for the brows of Mr. Hunt. Nearly eighty years ago, this pilgrimage of boyish enthusiasm—but a few months after Waterloo, the last rumblings of the long European wars still dying away in the distance. Our unhappy contest with that great, young republic, which you, Sir, so gracefully represent to-day, just over and done with. How long ago it seems, this page of history! How dusty and shadowy; and how fresh and near, across the face of it, the visit of the boyish poet to his friend and master on the hill of Hampstead!

Such, at all events, was the earliest appearance of Keats in this place, and here the "prosperous opening" of his poetical career was made. Here he first met Shelley, Haydon, and perhaps Wordsworth. Hence, in 1817, from under these pleasant trees and the "leafy luxury" of the Vale-of-Health his earliest volume was sent forth to the world. Here, in lodgings of his own in Well Walk, he settled in the same summer, that he might devote himself to the composition of *Endymion*. Here his best friends clustered round him—Bailey and Cowden Clarke, Dilke and Armitage Brown, and Reynolds. Here it was that, in the autumn of 1818, he met at Wentworth Place that brisk and shapely lady whose fascination was to make the cup of his sorrows overflow; hence it was, too, that on the 18th of September, 1820, he started for Italy, a dying man. All of Keats that is vivid and intelligent, all that is truly characteristic of his genius and his vitality, is centred around Hampstead, and you, his latest Western friends, have shown a fine instinct in bringing here, and not elsewhere, the gifts and tributes of your love.

If we find it easy to justify the locality which you have chosen for your monument to Keats, it is surely not less easy, although more serious and more elaborate, to bring forward reasons for the existence of that monument itself. In the first place, that you should so piously have prepared, and that we so eagerly, and so unanimously accept, a marble effigy of Keats—what does it signify, if not that we and and you alike acknowledge the fame that it represents to be durable, stimulating, and exalted? For, consider with me for a moment how singularly unattached is the reputation of this, our Hampstead poet. It rests upon no privilege of birth, no "stake in the country," as we say; it is fostered by no alliance of powerful friends, or wide circle of personal influences; no one living to-day has seen Keats, or artificially preserves his memory for any private purpose. In all but verse his name was, as he said, "writ in water." He is identified with no progression of ideas, no religious, or political, or social propaganda. He is either a poet, or absolutely nothing—we withdraw the poetical elements from our conception of him; and what is left? The palest phantom of a livery-stablekeeper's son, an unsuccessful medical student, an ineffectual, consumptive lad, who died in obscurity, more than seventy years ago.

You will forgive me for reminding you of this absence of all secondary qualities, of all outer accomplishments of life, in the career of that great man, whom we celebrate to-day, because, in so doing, I exalt the one primary quality which raised him among the principalities and powers of the human race, and makes our celebration of him to-day perfectly rational and explicable to all instructed men and women. It is not every one who appreciates poetry. It may be that such appreciation is really a somewhat rare and sequestered gift. But all practical men can understand that honour is due to those who have performed a difficult and noble task with superlative distinction. We may be no politicians, but we can comprehend the enthusiasm excited by a consummate statesman. Be it a sport or a profession, an art or a discovery, all men and women can acquiesce in the praise which is due to him who has exercised it the best out of a thousand who have attempted it. This, then, would be your answer to any who should question the propriety of your zeal or of our gratitude to-day. We are honouring John Keats, we should reply in unison, because he did with superlative charm and skill a thing which mankind has agreed to include among the noblest and most elevated occupations of the human intelligence. We honour, in the lad who passed so long unobserved among the inhabitants of Hampstead, a poet, and nothing but a poet, but one of the very greatest poets that the modern world has seen.

The Professor of Poetry at Oxford reminds me that Tennyson was more than once heard to assert that Keats, had his life been prolonged, would have been our greatest poet since Milton. This conviction is one now open to discussion, of course, but fit to be propounded in any assemblage of competent judges. It may be stated, at least, and yet the skies not fall upon our heads. Fifty years ago to have made such a proposition in public would have been thought ridiculous, and sixty years ago almost wicked. When the late Lord Houghton—a name so dear to many present, a name never to be mentioned without sympathy in any collection of literary persons—when Monckton Milnes, as in 1848 he still was, published his delightful life of Keats, it was widely looked upon as a rash and fantastic act to concentrate so much attention on so imperfect a career. But all that is over now. Keats lives, as he modestly assured his friends would be the case, among the English poets. Nor among them, merely, but in the first rank of them—among the very few of whom we instinctively think whenever the characteristic versemen of our race are spoken of.

To what does he owe his pre-eminence—he, the boy in this assemblage of strong men and venerable greybeards, he who had ceased to sing at an age when most of them were still practising their prosodical scales? To answer this adequately would take us much too far afield for a short address, the object of which is simply to acknowledge with decency your amiable gift. But some brief answer I must essay to make. Originality of poetic style was not, it seems to me, the predominant characteristic of Keats. It might have come with ripening years, but it cannot be at all certain that it would. It never came to Pope or to Lamartine, to Virgil or to Tennyson. It has come to poets infinitely the inferiors of these, infinitely the inferiors of Keats. Those who strive after direct originality forget that to be unlike those who have preceded us, in all the forms and methods of expression, is not by any means certainly to be either felicitous or distinguished. There is hardly any excellent feature in the poetry of Keats which is not superficially the feature of some well-recognised master of an age precedent to his own. He boldly takes down, as from some wardrobe of beautiful and diverse raiment, the dress of Spenser, of Milton, of Homer, of Ariosto, of Fletcher, and wears each in turn, thrown over shoulders which completely change its whole appearance and proportion. But, if he makes use of modes which are already familiar to us, in their broad outlines, as the modes invented by earlier masters, it is mainly because his temperament was one which imperatively led him to select the best of all possible forms of expression. His excursions into other people's provinces were always undertaken with a view to the annexation of the richest and most fertile acres.

It is comparatively vain to speculate as to the future of a man whose work was all done between the ages of nineteen and four-and-twenty. Yet I think we may see that what Keats was rapidly progressing towards, until the moment when his health gave way, was a crystallisation into one fused and perfect style of all the best elements of the poetry of the ages. When we think of Byron, we see that he would probably have become absorbed in the duties of the ruler of a nation; in Shelley, we conjecture that all was being merged in the politician and the humanitarian; but in Keats poetry was ever steadily and exclusively ascendant. Shall I say what will startle you if I confess that I sometimes fancy that we lost in the author of the five great odes the most masterful capacity for poetic expression which the world has ever seen?

Be this as it may, without vain speculation we may agree that we possess even in this fragment of work, in this truncated performance, one of the most splendid inheritances of English literature. "I have loved the principle of beauty in all things," Keats most truly said, "the mighty abstract idea of beauty in all things." It is this passion for intellectual beauty—less disturbed perhaps by distracting aims in him than in any other writer of all time—that sets the crown on our conception of his poetry. When he set out upon his mission, as a boy of twenty, he entered that "Chamber of Maiden Thought" of which he speaks to Reynolds, where he became intoxicated with the light and the atmosphere.

Many of his warmest admirers seem to have gone with him no further, to have stayed there among the rich colours and the Lydian melodies and the enchanting fresh perfumes. But the real Keats evades them if they pass no further. He had already risen to graver and austerer things, he had already bowed his shoulders under the burden of the mystery. But even in those darker galleries and up those harsher stairs he took one lamp with him, the light of harmonious thought. The profound and exquisite melancholy of his latest verse is permeated with this conception of the loftiest beauty as the only consolation in our jarring and bewildered world:

> *Beauty is truth, truth beauty—that is all*
> *Ye know on earth, and all ye need to know.*

And now, Sir, we turn again to you and to the gracious gift you bring us. In one of his gay moods Keats wrote to his brother George in Kentucky: "If I had a prayer to make, it should be that one of your children should be the first American poet." That wish was not realised; the "little child o' the western wild" remained, I believe, resolutely neglectful of the lyre its uncle offered to it. But the prophecies of great poets are fulfilled in divers ways, and in a broader sense all the recent poets of America are of Keats's kith and kin. Not one but has felt his influence; not one but has been swayed by his passion for the ethereal beauty; not one but is proud to recognise his authority and dignity.

The ceremony of to-day, so touching and so significant, is really, therefore, the pilgrimage of long-exiled children to what was once the home of their father.

THOMAS LOVELL BEDDOES

Thomas Lovell Beddoes

In a letter written to Kelsall in 1824, Beddoes makes the following remarks on the poetical situation of the moment:

" The disappearance of Shelley from the world seems, like the tropical setting of that luminary to which his poetical genius can alone be compared, with reference to the companions of his day, to have been followed by instant darkness and owl-season; whether the vociferous Darley is to be the comet, or tender full-faced L. E. L. the milk-and-watery moon of our darkness, are questions for the astrologers; if I were the literary weather-guesser for 1825 I would safely prognosticate fog, rain, blight in due succession for its dullard months."

When these words were written, the death of Byron four months previously had closed, for English readers, a romantic phase of our national verse. If Keats, Shelley, and Byron, however, were gone, it may be objected that all the other great poets of the age survived. This is true in a physical sense, but how many of them were still composing verse of any brilliant merit? Not

Coleridge, long ago stricken dumb to verse ; not Wordsworth, prosing on without the stimulus of inspiration ; even Moore or Southey were vocal no longer ; Campbell and Scott had practically taken farewell of the Muse. English poetry had been in blossom from 1795 to 1820 but the marvellous bloom was over, and the petals were scattered on the grass.

The subject of this memoir began to write at the very moment of complete exhaustion, when the age was dazzled with excess of genius, and when the nation was taking breath for a fresh burst of song. He had the misfortune to be a young man when Keats and Shelley were just dead, and when Tennyson and Browning were schoolboys. In the words which have just been quoted he has given a humorous view of the time, which shows that, at the age of twenty-one, he had grasped its characteristics. Among his exact contemporaries there was no one, except Praed, who was some months his senior, who inherited anything like genius. Beddoes was four years younger than Hood, two years older than Elizabeth Barrett. No other name has survived worthy of being even named beside his as a poet, except Macaulay, with whom he has nothing in common. He was early dissuaded from the practice of verse, and all that he has left, which is of any sterling value, was composed between 1821, when he published *The Improvisatore*, and 1826, when he practically finished *Death's Jest-Book*. He belongs to those five years of exhaustion and mediocrity, and the effect of having to write at such a period, there can be no doubt, dwarfed, restrained, and finally quenched his poetical faculty. It is not saying much, yet it is mere justice to insist, that Beddoes was, during those five years, the most interesting talent engaged in writing English verse.

II

Thomas Lovell Beddoes was born in Rodney Place, Clifton, on the 20th of July, 1803. He was the eldest son of a celebrated physician, Dr. Thomas Beddoes, who died in 1809, and left his son to the guardianship of Davies Giddy, afterwards known as Sir Davies Gilbert, P.R.S., who lived for thirty years longer. The boy's mother, Anna, was a sister of Maria Edgeworth, the novelist. He was educated at Bath Grammar School and at the Charterhouse, where, as early as 1817, he began to write verses. Of his character at school, where he showed signs at once of that eccentricity and independence of manners which were to distinguish him through life, a schoolfellow, Mr. C. D. Bevan, has preserved a very entertaining account, from which this short extract may be given:

"He knew Shakespeare well when I first saw him, and during his stay at the Charterhouse made himself master of all the best English dramatists, from Shakespeare's time, or before it, to the plays of the day. He liked acting, and was a good judge of it, and used to give apt though burlesque imitations of the popular actors, particularly of Kean and Macready. Though his voice was harsh and his enunciation offensively conceited, he read with so much propriety of expression and manner that I was always glad to listen : even when I was pressed into the service as his accomplice, or his enemy, or his love, with a due accompaniment of curses, caresses, or kicks, as the course of his declamation required. One play in particular, Marlow's tragedy of *Dr. Faustus*, excited my admiration, and was fixed on my memory in this way."

At school he came under the influence of Fielding, and wrote a novel, entitled *Cynthio and Bugboo*, the loss of which we need scarcely deplore, as, according to the same authority, it was marked by "all the coarseness, little of the wit, and none of the truth of his original." The fragments of his schoolboy verse, in particular the rhapsody of *Alfarabi*, display a very singular adroitness in the manufacture of easy blank verse, and precocious tendency to a species of mocking metaphysics, both equally unlike a child. In July, 1819, while still at Charterhouse, a sonnet of his was printed in the *Morning Post*. On the 1st of May, 1820, Beddoes proceeded to Oxford, and was entered a commoner at Pembroke, which had been his father's college.

Although he had been a forward boy at school, Beddoes passed through Oxford without any academic distinction. He was a freshman of eighteen when, in 1821, he published his first volume, *The Improvisatore*, of which he afterwards carefully tried to destroy every copy. In 1822 he published, as another thin pamphlet, *The Brides' Tragedy*, which has also become extremely rare. These two little books, the work of an undergraduate less than twenty years of age, are the only ones which Beddoes ever published. The remainder of his writings, whether lyrical or dramatic, were issued posthumously, not less than thirty years later. *The Brides' Tragedy* attracted some notice in literary circles; it secured for the young Oxford poet the friendship of a man much older than himself, but of kindred tastes, Bryan Waller Procter. The dramatic poems of "Barry Cornwall," of which *Mirandola* was then the latest, had been appearing in rapid succession, and their amiable author was a person of considerable influence. It was Procter who, in 1823, introduced Beddoes to Thomas Forbes Kelsall, a young lawyer practising at Southampton. It had been thought well that Beddoes, who was sadly behind-hand with his studies, should go down to this quiet town to read for his bachelor's degree, and he remained at Southampton for some months, in great intimacy with Kelsall, and forming no other acquaintance.

While he was at Southampton, Beddoes wrote a great deal of desultory verse, almost all of a dramatic order; to this period belong *The Second Brother* and *Torrismond*, among other fragments. Already he was seized with that inability to finish, that lack of an organic principle of poetical composition, which were to prevent him from mounting to those heights of which his facility and brilliancy seem to promise him an easy ascent. The death of Shelley appears to have drawn his attention to the genius of that writer, by which he was instantly fascinated, and, as it were, absorbed.

Outside the small circle of Shelley's personal friends, Beddoes was perhaps the first to appreciate the magnitude of his merit, as he was certainly the earliest to imitate Shelley's lyrical work. His letters to Procter and Kelsall are full of evidence of his over-mastering passion for Shelley, and it was to Beddoes, in the first instance, that the publication of that writer's *Posthumous Poems* was due. In the winter of 1823 Beddoes started a subscription with his two friends, and corresponded with John Hunt on the subject. They promised to take 250 copies, but Hunt said that Mrs. Shelley ought to have some profit. This seemed hardly fair to Beddoes; "for the twinkling of this very distant chance we, three poor honest admirers of Shelley's poetry, are certainly to pay." At this time Beddoes was writing two romantic dramas, *Love's Arrow Poisoned* and *The Last Man*, both founded on the tragic model of Webster, Cyril Tourneur, and Middleton. Of these plays not very much was ever written, and still less is now in existence. Of *The Last Man* he writes, in February 1824: "There are now three first acts in my drawer. When I have got two more, I shall stitch them together, and stick the sign of a fellow tweedling a mask in his fingers, with 'good entertainment for man and ass' understood."

The year 1824 he spent in London, Oxford, and Bristol. Already his eccentric shyness had grown upon him. He writes to Kelsall from his lodgings in Devereux Court, Temple, March 29, 1824:

"Being a little shy, and not a little proud perhaps,

I have held back and never made the first step towards discovering my residence or existence to any of my family friends [in London]. In consequence I have lived in a deserted state, which I could hardly bear much longer without sinking into that despondency on the brink of which I have sate so long. Your cheerful presence at times (could we not mess together occasionally?) would set me up a good deal, but perhaps you had better not draw my heavy company on your head. . . . . I met an intelligent man who had lived at Hampstead, seen Keats, and was read in his and the poems of Shelley. On my mentioning the former by accident to him, he complimented me on my similarity of countenance; he did not think much of K.'s genius, and therefore did not say it insincerely or sycophantically. The same was said by Procter and Taylor before."

Mrs. Procter, who had known both poets, made the same remark about Beddoes to myself; but she added that she never saw in the latter the extraordinary look of inspiration which was occasionally to be detected in the great eyes of Keats.

In the summer of 1824 Beddoes was hastily called to Florence by the illness of his mother, who was living there. She died before he could reach her, but he spent some weeks there, saw Walter Savage Landor, and then returned to Clifton in charge of his sisters. In October of the same year he began to study German, a language then but little known in this country. He attacked it languidly at first, then with ever-increasing eagerness and zest. But the Elizabethan drama was still his principal delight, and he studied it, even in its least illustrious forms, with extraordinary closeness and gusto. Writing to Kelsall from Clifton (January 11, 1825), he remarks, àpropos of a revival of *The Fatal Dowry* of Massinger:

"Say what you will, I am convinced the man who is to awaken the drama must be a bold trampling fellow—no creeper into worm-holes—no reviver even, however good. These reanimations are vampire-cold. Such ghosts as Marloe, Webster, &c., are better dramatists, better poets, I dare say, than any contemporary of ours, but they are ghosts—the worm is in their pages—and we want to see something that our great-grandsires did not know. With the greatest reverence for all the antiquities of the drama, I still think that we had better beget than revive, attempt to give the literature of this age an idiosyncracy and spirit of its own, and only raise a ghost to gaze on, not to live with. Just now the drama is a haunted ruin. I am glad that you are awakening to a sense of Darley. He must have no little perseverance to have gone through so much of that play; it will perchance be the first star of a new day."

The result of so much meditation on the drama was the composition of more fragments. *The Second Brother*, *Torrismond*, and *The Last Man* occupied Beddoes during the winter and spring of 1824–5. But none of these approached completion. He then planned the publication of a volume of lyrics, to be entitled

Outidana, or Effusions, amorous, pathetic, and fantastical, which was to include most of the miscellaneous verses reprinted in 1890, and others which are now lost. On the 25th of May, 1825, Beddoes took an ordinary bachelor's degree at Oxford. He writes to Kelsall from Pembroke College, on the 8th of June, announcing for the first time the most celebrated of his writings:

"Oxford is the most indolent place on earth. I have fairly done nothing in the world but read a play or two of Schiller, Æschylus and Euripides—you I suppose read German now as fast as English. I do not finish that 2nd Brother you saw but am thinking of a very Gothic-styled tragedy for which I have a jewel of a name:

DEATH'S JESTBOOK—

of course no one will ever read it. Mr. Milman (our poetry professor) has made me quite unfashionable here by denouncing me as one of a 'villainous school.' I wish him another son."

He now suddenly determined to abandon literature, which had suggested itself to him as a profession, and take up the study of medicine. We find him, therefore, on the 19th of July, 1825, at Hamburg, "sitting on a horse-hair sofa, looking over the Elbe, with his meerschaum at his side, full of Grave, and abundantly prosaic. To-morrow, according to the prophecies of the diligence, he will set out for Hanover, and by the end of this week mein Herr Thomas will probably be a Doctor of the University of Göttingen." This, however, was rather premature. He did not become a doctor until much later. It is important to observe that the exodus to Germany thus casually and nonchalantly taken involved nothing less, as it proved, than a complete alteration in all his habits. Except for very few and brief visits, he did not return to England for the rest of his life, and he so completely adopted the language and thoughts of a German student as almost to cease to be an Englishman.

At Göttingen the celebrated man of science, Prof. Blumenbach, became the most intimate friend of Beddoes. The latter threw himself with the utmost ardour into the study of physiology and medicine. He did not, however, at first abandon his design of becoming an English dramatic poet. He writes to Kelsall (Dec. 4, 1825):

"I am perhaps somewhat independent, and have a competence adequate to my philosophical desires. There are reasons why I should reject too much practice if it did intrude; really I am much more likely to remain a patientless physician. And now I will end this unnecessary subject, by telling you that *Death's Jestbook* goes on like the tortoise, slow and sure; I think it will be entertaining, very unamiable, and utterly unpopular. Very likely it may be finished in the spring or autumn."

His misanthropy, for it almost deserves so harsh a name, grew upon him. "I feel myself," he wrote, "in a measure alone in the world and likely to remain so, for, from the experiments I have made, I fear I am a non-conductor of friendship, a not-very-likeable person, so that I must make sure of my own respect, and occupy that part of the brain which should be employed in imaginative attachments in the pursuit of immaterial and unchanging good." In April, 1826, *Death's Jestbook* is still lying "like a snow-ball, and I give it a kick every now and then, out of mere scorn and ill-humour; the 4th act, and I may say the 5th, are more than half done, so that at last it will be a perfect mouse, but such doggerell!" None the less did he anticipate that the poem would come "like an electric shock among the small critics." In October, 1826, it is "done and done for, its limbs being as scattered and unconnected as those of the old gentleman whom Medea minced and boiled young. I have tried 20 times at least to copy it fair." He intended at this time to send the MS. to Kelsall and Procter to be seen through the press, but he delayed until he could bring the poem himself to London.

His monotonous existence in Göttingen was broken in the spring of 1828 by a visit of a few days to England, where he took his degree of M.A. at Oxford, and hurried back to Germany. Meanwhile he had left *Death's Jestbook* with Procter and Kelsall for publication, but they decided that it must be "revised and improved." In his fifth year in Germany, "having already been at Göttingen the time which it is allowed for any student to remain there," he transferred his residence to Würzburg, in Bavaria; "a very clever professor of medicine and capital midwife brought me here, and a princely hospital." In 1831 there was again some abortive talk of publishing *Death's Jestbook.* About this time Beddoes became more and more affected by opinions of the extreme radical order; he subscribed towards "the support of candidates who were professed supporters of the Reform Bill," and he began to affect a warm personal interest in certain revolutionary Poles who had taken up their abode in Würzburg. He continued his medical studies with great thoroughness, and in the summer of 1832 he took his degree of doctor of medicine in the University, being now in his thirtieth year. He was more and more mixed up in political intrigue, and on the 25th of September, 1832, he somewhat obscurely says:

"The absurdity of the King of Bavaria has cost me a good deal, as I was obliged to oppose every possible measure to the arbitrary illegality of his conduct, more for the sake of future objects of his petty royal malice than my own, of course in vain."

He was soon after obliged to fly, "banished by that ingenious Jackanapes of Bavaria," in common with several of his distinguished Würzburg friends. He took refuge, first in Strassburg, then in Zurich. He brought with him to Switzerland a considerable reputation as a physiologist, for Blumenbach, in a testimonial which exists, calls him the best pupil he ever had. It appears that he now assumed, what he afterwards dropped, the degree of M.D., and had some practice as a physician in the town of Zurich. In 1835 the surgeon Schoenlien proposed Beddoes to the medical faculty of the University as professor of Comparative Anatomy, and the latter unanimously seconded him. His election, however, was not ratified, according to one of his letters, for political reasons, according to another because he was found to be ineligible, from his having published nothing of a medical character. He spent several healthy and tolerably happy years in Zurich, "what," he says in March, 1837, "with a careless temper and the pleasant translunary moods I walk and row myself into upon the lakes and over the Alps of Switzerland;" and once more, as he quaintly put it, he began "to brew small ale out of the water of the fountain of the horse's foot," working again on the revision of *Death's Jestbook*. He also began to prepare for the press a collection of his narrative and lyrical poems, to be called *The Ivory Gate*. In 1838 he was engaged in translating Grainger's work on the Spinal Cord into German.

He had spent six years at Zurich, and was beginning to feel that city to have become his settled home, when, on the 8th of September, 1839, a political catastrophe destroyed his peace of mind. A mob of six thousand peasants, "half of them unarmed, and the other half armed with scythes, dung-forks and poles, led on by a mad fanatic and aided by some traitors in the cabinet, and many in the town," stormed Zurich, and upset the liberal government of the canton. Beddoes observed the riot from a window, and witnessed the murder of the minister Hegetschweiler, who was one of his best friends. He wrote: "In consequence of this state of things, in which neither property nor person is secure,

I shall find it necessary to give up my present residence entirely. Indeed, the dispersion of my friends and acquaintance, all of whom belonged to the liberal party, renders it nearly impossible for me to remain longer here." He loitered on, however, until March, 1840, when his life was threatened by the insurgents, and he was helped to fly from Zurich in secret by a former leader of the liberal party, whom he had befriended, a man of the name of Jasper.

It is probable that the seven years Beddoes spent at Zurich formed the happiest portion of his life. He was never to experience tranquillity again. The next few years were spent in what seems an aimless wandering through the length and breadth of Central Europe. Little is known of his history from this time forward. In 1841 he was in Berlin, where he formed an acquaintanceship with a young Dr. Frey, who remained his intimate friend to the last. In 1842 he made a brief visit to England. In 1843 he went to Baden in Aargau, where he seems to have stored his library, and, so far as Beddoes henceforth could be said to have a home, that home was in this little town of Northern Switzerland, not far from Zurich. He spent the winter of 1844 at Giessen, attracted thither by Liebig and his famous school of chemistry, after having lodged through the summer and autumn at Basel, Strassburg, Mannheim, Mainz, and Frankfurt in succession. At Giessen a little of the poetic fervour returned to him, and it was here that he wrote " The Swallow leaves her Nest," and " In Lover's Ear a wild Voice cried." But most of his verse now was written in German. He says (Nov. 13, 1844): "Sometimes to amuse myself I write a German lyric or epigram, right scurrilous, many of which have appeared in the Swiss and German papers, and some day or other I shall have them collected and printed for fun." It is needless to say that he never issued this collection, and the German poems, doubtless signed with a pseudonym or else anonymous, have never been traced.

In August, 1846, he came to England for a considerable stay. Intending to remain six weeks, he loitered on for ten months. His friends, few of whom had seen him for more than twenty years, found him altered beyond all recognition. He had become extremely rough and cynical in speech, and eccentric in manners. I am informed by a member of his family that he arrived at the residence of one of his relations, Cheney Longville, near Ludlow, astride the back of a donkey. He complained of neuralgia, and for six out of the ten months which he spent in England, he was shut up in a bedroom, reading and smoking, and admitting no visitor. In April, 1847, he went down to Fareham, to stay with Mr. Kelsall, and this greatly brightened him up. From Fareham he proceeded in May to London, and there he met with his old friends the Procters. From Mrs. Procter the present writer received a graphic account of his manners and appearance. She told me that his eccentricities were so marked that they almost gave the impression of insanity, but that closer observation showed them to be merely the result of a peculiar fancy, entirely unaccustomed to restraint, and of the occasional rebound of spirits after a period of depression. The Procters found Beddoes a most illusive companion. He would come to them uninvited, but never if he had been asked, or if he feared to meet a stranger. On one occasion, Mrs. Procter told me, they had asked Beddoes to dine with them, and proceed afterwards to Drury Lane Theatre. He did not come, and they dined alone. On approaching the theatre, they saw Beddoes in charge of the police, and on inquiry found that he had just been arrested for trying to put Drury Lane on fire. The incendiary, however, had used no more dangerous torch than a five-pound note, and Mr. Procter had little difficulty in persuading the police that this was much more likely to hurt the pocket of Mr. Beddoes than the rafters of the theatre.

In June, 1847, Beddoes returned to Frankfurt, where he lived until the spring of 1848 with a baker named Degen, who was then about nineteen years of age—"a nice-looking young man dressed in a blue blouse, fine in expression, and of a natural dignity of manner," Miss Zoë King describes him. While Beddoes was in Frankfurt his blood became poisoned from the virus of a dead body entering a slight wound in his hand. This was overcome, but it greatly weakened and depressed him. For six months he would see no one but Degen. He complained of disgust of life, and declared that his republican friends in Germany had deserted him. He persuaded Degen to become an actor, and he occupied himself in teaching him English and other accomplishments, cutting himself off from all other company. At this time "he had let his beard grow, and looked like Shakespeare." In May, 1848, he left Frankfurt, inducing Degen to accompany him, and the two companions wandered together through Germany and Switzerland. In Zurich Beddoes chartered the theatre for one night, to give his friend an opportunity of appearing in the part of Hotspur.

For about six weeks, so far as it is possible to discover, Beddoes was tolerably happy. But he was separated from Degen at Basel, where Beddoes took a room, in a condition of dejected apathy that was pitiful to witness, at the Cicogne Hôtel. Here very early next morning he inflicted a deep wound on his right leg, with a razor. "Il était miserable—il a voulu se tuer," as the waiter who attended upon him said afterwards to Miss Zoë King. He was, however, removed with success to the Town Hospital, where his friends Dr. Frey and Dr. Ecklin waited upon him. He had a pleasant private room, looking into a large garden. He communicated with his English friends, being very anxious to allay all suspicion. He wrote to his sister: "In July I fell with a horse in a precipitous part of the neighbouring hills, and broke my left leg all to pieces." He begged no one in England to be anxious, and his version of the catastrophe was accepted without question. The leg, however, was obstinate in recovery, for the patient stealthily tore off the bandages, and eventually gangrene of the foot set in. On the 9th of September it became necessary to amputate the leg below the knee-joint; this operation was very successfully performed by Dr. Ecklin. Beddoes seems to have been cheerful during the autumn months, and Degen came back to Basel, lodging near him in the town. The poet gave up all suicidal attempts, and it was considered that his mind on this matter was completely cured. His bed was covered with books, and he conversed and wrote freely about literature and science. He talked of going to Italy when he was convalescent, and in December he walked out of his room twice. The first time he went out into the town, however, on the 26th of January, 1849, he seems to have used his authority as a physician to procure the deadly poison called Kurara; in the course of the evening Dr. Ecklin was suddenly called to his bedside, and found the poet lying on his back insensible, with the following extraordinary note, written in pencil, folded on his bosom. It was addressed to one of the oldest of his English friends, Mr. R. Phillips:

"MY DEAR PHILLIPS,—I am food for what I am good for—worms. I have made a will here, which I desire to be respected; and add the donation of £20 to Dr. Ecklin my physician. W. Beddoes must have a case (50 bottles) of Champagne Moet 1847 growth to drink my death in. Thanks for all kindnesses. Borrow the £200. You are a good and noble man, and your children must look sharp to be like you.—Yours, if my own, ever   "T. L. B.

"Love to Anna, Henry,—the Beddoes of Longvill
and Zoë and Emmeline King. Also to Kelsall, whom
I beg to look at my MSS. and print or not as *he* thinks
fit. I ought to have been, [among a] variety of other
things, a good poet. Life was too great a bore on one
peg, and that a bad one. Buy for Dr. Ecklin above
mentioned Reade's best stomach-pump."

He died at 10 P.M. the same night, and was buried
under a cypress in the cemetery of the hospital. The
circumstances of his death, now for the first time published, were ascertained by Miss Zoë King, who visited
Basel in 1857, and saw Degen, Frey, Ecklin, and the
people at the Cicogne Hôtel. After some delay, the
various MSS. of Beddoes were placed in Kelsall's hands,
and that faithful and admirable friend published that
version of *Death's Jestbook*, which seemed to him the
most attractive, in 1850; and this he followed, in 1851,
by the *Miscellaneous Poems*, with an unsigned Memoir.
These two volumes form the only monument hitherto
raised to the memory of the unfortunate poet. The
reception which was given to them was respectful, and
even sympathetic. It may be sufficient here to give
one instance of it, which has never been made public.
Miss Zoë King, in an unprinted letter to Kelsall,
says: "I was at the Lakes with my uncle Edgeworth just after receiving the *Death's Jestbook*, and
was very much pleased to lend it to Mr. Tennyson. He was just arrived (and at a distance from us)
on his wedding tour, so that I merely *saw* him. He

returned the book with a few lines of praise, rating it highly."

III

It is not in the fragments that Beddoes has left behind him that we can look for the work of a full-orbed and serene poetical genius. It would be a narrow definition indeed of the word "poet" which should exclude him, but he belongs to the secondary order of makers. He is not one of those whose song flows unbidden from their lips, those born warblers whom neither poverty, nor want of training, nor ignorance, can restrain from tuneful utterance. He belongs to the tribe of scholar-poets, to the educated artists in verse. In every line that he wrote we can trace the influence of existing verse upon his mind. He is intellectual rather than spontaneous. Nor, even within this lower range, does his work extend far on either hand. He cultivates a narrow field, and his impressions of life and feeling are curiously limited and monotonous. At the feast of the Muses he appears bearing little except one small savoury dish, some cold preparation, we may say, of olives and anchovies, the strangeness of which has to make up for its lack of importance. Not every palate enjoys this *hors d'œuvre*, and when that is the case, Beddoes retires; he has nothing else to give. He appeals to a few literary epicures, who, however, would deplore the absence of this oddly flavoured dish as much as that of any more important *pièce de resistance*.

As a poet, the great defect of Beddoes has already been indicated—his want of sustained invention, his powerlessness in evolution. He was poor just where, two hundred years earlier, almost every playwright in the street had been strong, namely, in the ability to conduct an interesting story to a thrilling and appropriate close. From this point of view his boyish play, *The Brides' Tragedy*, is his only success. In this case a story was developed with tolerable skill to a dramatic ending. But, with one exception, he never again could contrive to drag a play beyond a certain point; in the second or third act its wings would droop, and it would expire, do what its master would. These unfinished tragedies were like those children of Polynesian dynasties, anxiously trained, one after another, in the warm Pacific air, yet ever doomed to fall, on the borders of manhood, by the breath of the same mysterious disease. *Death's Jestbook* is but an apparent exception. This does indeed appear in the guise of a finished five-act play; but its completion was due to the violent determination of its author, and not to legitimate inspiration. For many years, in and out of season, Beddoes, who had pledged his whole soul to the finishing of this book, assailed it with all the instruments of his art, and at last produced a huge dramatic Frankenstein monster, which, by adroit editing, could be forced into the likeness of a tragedy. But no play in literature was less of a spontaneous creation, or was further from achieving the ideal of growing like a tree.

From what Beddoes was not, however, it is time to

pass to what he was. In several respects, then, he was a poetical artist of consummate ability. Of all the myriad poets and poeticules who have tried to recover the lost magic of the tragic blank verse of the Elizabethans, Beddoes has come nearest to success. If it were less indifferent to human interests of every ordinary kind, the beauty of his dramatic verse would not fail to fascinate. To see how strong it is, how picturesque, how admirably fashioned, we have only to compare it with what others have done in the same style, with the tragic verse, for instance, of Barry Cornwall, of Talfourd, of Horne. But Beddoes is what he himself has called "a creeper into worm-holes." He attempts nothing personal; he follows the very tricks of Marston and Cyril Tourneur like a devoted disciple. The passions with which he deals are remote and unfamiliar; we may go further, and say that they are positively obsolete.

In another place I have compared Beddoes in poetry with the Helsche Breughel in painting. He dedicates himself to the service of Death, not with a brooding sense of the terror and shame of mortality, but from a love of the picturesque pageantry of it, the majesty and sombre beauty, the swift, theatrical transitions, the combined elegance and horror that wait upon the sudden decease of monarchs. His medical taste and training encouraged this tendency to dwell on the physical aspects of death, and gave him a sort of ghastly familiarity with images drawn from the bier and the charnel-house. His attitude, however, though cold and cynical, was always distinguished, and in his wildest flights of humour he commonly escapes vulgarity. In this he shows himself a true poet. As we read his singular pages, we instinctively expect to encounter that touch of prose which, in Landor's phrase, will precipitate the whole, yet it never comes. Beddoes often lacks inspiration, but distinction he can never be said to lack.

As a lyrist he appears, on the whole, to rank higher than as a dramatist. Several of his songs, artificial as they are, must always live, and take a high place in the literature of artifice. As a writer of this class of poem his experience of the Elizabethans was further kindled and largely modified by the example of Shelley. Nevertheless his finest songs could never be taken for the work of Shelley, or, indeed, attributed to any hand but his own. Among them, the song in *Torrismond* is perhaps the sweetest and the most ingenious:

> *How many times do I love thee, dear!*
> *Tell me how many thoughts there be*
> *In the atmosphere*
> *Of a new fall'n year*
> *Whose white and sable hours appear*
> *The latest flake of Eternity:*
> *So many times do I love thee, dear.*
>
> *How many times do I love, again!*
> *Tell me how many beads there are*
> *In a silver chain*
> *Of evening rain,*
> *Unravalled from the tumbling main,*
> *And threading the eye of a silver star:*
> *So many times do I love, again.*

Dream Pedlary the most exquisite:

DREAM-PEDLARY.

If there were dreams to sell,
  What would you buy?
Some cost a passing bell,
  Some a light sigh,
That shakes from Life's fresh crown
Only a rose leaf down.
If there were dreams to sell,
Merry and sad to tell,
And the crier rung the bell,
  What would you buy?

A cottage lone and still
  With bowers nigh,
Shadowy, my woes to still
  Until I die:
Such pearl from Life's fresh crown
Fain would I shake me down:
Were dreams to have at will,
This would best heal my ill,
  This would I buy.

The *Song of the Stygian Naiades* and *Old Adam, the Carrion Crow*, are instances of fancy combined with grisly humour, of a class in which Beddoes has no English competitor. The Harpagus ballad in the fourth act of *Death's Jestbook*, and "Lord Alcohol," which I printed for the first time in 1890, are less known, but no less vivid and extraordinary. The former of these closes in fierce stanzas, which Robert Browning almost extravagantly admired, and was never weary of reciting:

> *From the old supper-giver's poll,*
> *He tore the many-kingdomed mitre;*
> *To him, who cost him his son's soul,*
> *He gave it; to the Persian fighter:*
> *And quoth,*
> *Old art thou, but a fool in blood:*
> *If thou hast made me eat my son,*
> *Cyrus has ta'en his grandsire's food;*
> *There's kid for child, and who hath won?*
>
> *All kingdomless is thy old head,*
> *In which began the tyrannous fun;*
> *Thou'rt slave to him, who should be dead;*
> *There's kid for child, and who hath won?*

Beddoes possesses great sense of verbal melody, a fastidious ear, and considerable, though far from faultless, skill in metrical architecture. His boyish volume, called *The Improvisatore*, shows, despite its crudity, that these gifts were early developed. To say more in recommendation of Beddoes were needless. Those readers who are able to take pleasure in poetry so grim, austere, and abnormal, may safely be left to discover his specific charms for themselves.

1890.

BIBLIOGRAPHICAL NOTE.

During his own lifetime, with the exception of a few brief contributions to periodicals, Beddoes published nothing but two small volumes. One of these was *The Improvisatore*, issued at Oxford in 1821, and so successfully suppressed by its author, that not more than five or six copies are known to exist. It was reprinted for the first time in my 1890 edition, from a copy in the collection of Mr. J. Dykes Campbell. The other was *The Brides' Tragedy*, published by the Rivingtons in 1822. This is rare, though by no means so inaccessible as its predecessor. A second edition appeared in 1851. This play I reprinted from a copy of the 1822 original in my own library.

At the time of Beddoes' death in 1849 the bulk of his MSS. remained inedited. He specially bequeathed his papers and the disposal of them to Thomas Forbes Kelsall, a solicitor at Fareham, who was the oldest and the most intimate of his English friends. The family of the poet, whose knowledge of him had grown very slight, were at first exceedingly undesirous that his poetic MSS. should be preserved, although they were willing to pay for the publication of any scientific writings. Their repugnance was finally overcome, and in 1850 Kelsall published, in a thin volume, *Death's Jestbook*. The editing of this poem was no light task, for no fewer than three distinct texts, differing very considerably between themselves, were found to exist. Kelsall collated these three versions, and produced a selected text of his own, to which I in the main adhered. If the interest in Beddoes should continue to grow, it will always be possible to produce a variorum edition of *Death's Jestbook*, a demand for which, however, is hardly to be expected.

In 1851 Kelsall collected the miscellaneous poems and dramatic fragments into a volume entitled *Poems by the late Thomas Lovell Beddoes*, to which he prefixed an anonymous memoir of the poet, which is a model of loving care and respect for the memory of the departed; a man of whom it might then be said with unusual truth, that he was a bard "whom there were none to praise and very few to love." The result of Kelsall's zeal was that, for the first time, the poetry of Beddoes began to excite attention. Of *Death's Jestbook* very few copies had been sold, and it is extremely rare in that original condition. The sheets of this and of the *Poems* were rebound, with a new title-page ("The Poems, posthumous and collected, of Thomas Lovell Beddoes"), 1851, in two volumes, to the second of which *The Brides' Tragedy* was added. In this form Beddoes is usually known to collectors, but even these volumes are now difficult to procure. The remainder of them was dispersed by auction in 1855, since which time until 1890 Beddoes was out of print.

In 1853 Miss Zoë King, Beddoes' cousin, wrote to Kelsall: "I do not know whether I mentioned to you the high terms of praise with which both Mr. and Mrs. Browning spoke of the poems, just as they were published." Miss Zoë King preserved a romantic interest in T. L. Beddoes, although she, like every other member of his family, knew very little indeed about him personally. She wrote to Kelsall: "I could give you very little information of my early reminiscences of my poor Cousin, as I was so much in awe of his reserve and of his talents that I seldom conversed with him." It was, nevertheless, Miss King for whom Kelsall preserved the highest consideration, and her wishes were consulted in the next step which he took. He had religiously preserved every scrap of Beddoes' writing, and was anxious that these MSS. should be kept together. In consequence of Miss King's report of the admiration which the Brownings felt for Beddoes, and the fact that Robert Browning was the only English poet younger than himself in whom Beddoes took any interest, Kelsall made up his mind to make him the repository of the MSS. But he did not know him. Towards the close, however, of Bryan Waller Procter's life—I think in 1866 or 1867—Browning and Kelsall met at his house on one single occasion, and the latter then stated his request.

It is now proper to give the text of the papers by which Kelsall made the transfer of the Beddoes MSS. to Robert Browning:

"FAREHAM, *Sept.* 30, 1869.

"It is my wish that after my death, when and so soon as my wife may think proper, the whole of the Beddoes MSS. and papers should be transferred to Mr. Robert Browning, who has consented to accept the charge. It is most desirable, however, that she should look through them and remove the extraneous matter, as there are letters of other people, accounts, &c., which only swell the bulk without increasing the interest. Mr. Browning is to have Miss King's Journal from Switzerland and such of her letters as throw light on Beddoes' life or death. As to the latter, I have considered that my lips were sealed (relating to the suicide) during Miss King's lifetime, since such was her wish, altho' the fact has been communicated to me from an independent source. When my wife and I went to Basle in 1868, we visited Dr. Ecklin (Beddoes' much-esteemed physician), and found that he had no doubt as to the injuries which brought Beddoes to the hospital having been self-inflicted, and that accident there was none.

"He saw a good deal of Beddoes during his stay at the hospital before and after the amputation, and considered that in all their communications the origin of his situation was an understood fact between them. Dr. Ecklin added the startling information that the final catastrophe was, in his opinion, the direct result of a self-administered poison — all the symptoms being otherwise wholly unaccountable, and corresponding to those appropriate to the application of a very strong poison called Kurara or [blank in MS.]. He was evidently tired of life, and the fact of his being so, and of having achieved his release, need not, after a fair allowance for family hesitation, and in my opinion should not, be withheld from the knowledge of those who take a deep and true interest in Beddoes as a great poet.

"Thos. F. Kelsall."

To this paper succeeded another:

"I transfer to Robert Browning all my interests and authority in and over the MSS. and the papers of or concerning the poet Beddoes, for him to act discretionally for the honour of the poet.

"The greater portion of these MSS. was *given* by him to me in his life-time, and the remainder placed at my absolute disposal by his death-bed memorandum.

"T. F. Kelsall.

"Fareham, *June* 15, '72."

Shortly after this Mr. Kelsall died, and the box containing the Beddoes papers was transmitted to Mr Robert Browning. They remained locked up and unexamined until, in July, 1883, Mr. Browning invited me to help him in undertaking a complete investigation of the MSS. When we had reduced them to some order, he lent them to me, and I made such transcripts and collations as formed the basis of the edition of 1890. With regard to the circumstances of Beddoes' death, which were then for the first time made public, it was Mr. Browning's wish that Kelsall's instructions should be followed, at a proper interval after the death of Miss Zoë King, who was the last person to whom the statement could give any personal pain. Miss King died on Sept. 28, 1881, and I therefore judged that the time had arrived for carrying out Kelsall's directions. In 1893 I completed the task which my revered friend, Mr. Browning, had laid upon me, by printing the Correspondence of Beddoes, in a single volume.

In the preparation of all these volumes I received invaluable aid from another deeply regretted friend, Mr. J. Dykes Campbell, who was unequalled and perhaps unapproached in his knowledge of the late Georgian period of English poetical history. The Beddoes Papers remain in the possession of Mr. Robert Barrett Browning, who very kindly lent them to me again, that I might revise my collation.

EDWARD FITZGERALD

Edward FitzGerald

IN 1885 a great stimulus to curiosity about the translator of *Omar Khayyám* was given by the double inscription, prologue and epilogue, *ave atque vale*, in which Lord Tennyson put forth his *Tiresias* to the world under the shadow of the name of Edward FitzGerald. The curtain was for a moment drawn from the personality of one of the most recluse and sequestered of modern men of letters, and we saw, with the eyes of the Poet Laureate, one of the earliest and one of the most interesting of his associates:

> *Old Fitz, who from your suburb grange,*
>   *Where once I tarried for a while,*
> *Glance at the wheeling orb of change,*
>   *And greet it with a kindly smile;*
> *Whom yet I see as there you sit*
>   *Beneath your sheltering garden-tree,*
> *And watch your doves about you flit,*
>   *And plant on shoulder, hand and knee,*
> *Or on your head their rosy feet,*
>   *As if they knew your diet spares*
> *Whatever moved in that full sheet*
>   *Let down to Peter at his prayers;*
> *Who feed on milk and meal and grass."*

This dedication, as we now learn, had been written a week before FitzGerald's death, in June, 1883, when the intimacy of the two poets had lasted for nearly fifty years. Other friends, scarcely less dear or less admired, had already preceded FitzGerald to the grave. Thackeray, a little before the end, in reply to his daughter's inquiry which of his old friends he had loved most, had answered, "Why, dear old Fitz, to be sure." Carlyle growled at the comparative rarity of "your friendly human letters," and a few more—James Spedding, Thompson of Trinity, Crabbe, Bernard Barton—had tempted his woodland spirit from its haunts. But few indeed among the living can boast of having enjoyed even a slight personal acquaintanceship with Edward FitzGerald, and almost his only intimate friend now left is the editor of the *Letters and Literary Remains* (Macmillan & Co. : 3 vols.), which have revealed even to those who had placed FitzGerald's genius highest and studied him most carefully an unsuspected individuality of great force and charm. The learned and accomplished Vice-Master of Trinity has fulfilled his task in a manner almost too modest. He leaves FitzGerald to speak to us without a commentary from the pages of his matchless translations and from the leaves of his scarcely less delightful letters.

Edward Purcell was born in a Jacobean mansion at Bredfield, three miles from Woodbridge, in Suffolk, on the 31st of March, 1809. His father had married a Miss FitzGerald, and on the death of her father, in 1818, he assumed the name and arms of FitzGerald. The poet's childhood was spent in France, but at the age of thirteen he went to a school at Bury St. Edmunds, where the Speddings, W. B. Donne, and J. M. Kemble were among his schoolfellows. In 1826 he was entered at Trinity College, Cambridge, and in 1828 he formed the friendship of two freshmen, slightly younger than himself, who were to be his intimates for life, W. M. Thackeray and W. H. Thompson, lately Master of Trinity. He saw Lord Tennyson about this time, although he did not make his acquaintance until they left college; but half a century later he retained a clear recollection of the appearance of the Poet Laureate as an undergraduate—"I remember him well, a sort of Hyperion."

It is consistent with all that we learn of the shy fidelity of FitzGerald that almost all the friendships of his life were formed before he was one-and-twenty. As early as 1830 he warns Thackeray not to invite him to meet anybody; "I cannot stand seeing new faces in the polite circles;" and while the rest of the companionship, each in his own way, turned to conquer the world, FitzGerald remained obstinately and successfully obscure. In 1831 he was nearly caught, for a very delicate and fantastic lyric, published anonymously in the *Athenæum*, attracted remark and was attributed to Charles Lamb. FitzGerald took a farmhouse of his father's on the battle-field of Naseby, and paid no heed to the outstretched hands of the Sirens. He was in easy circumstances and adopted no profession. The seat of his family, and his own main residence until

1835, was Wherstead Lodge, a house beautifully placed on the west bank of the Orwell, about two miles from Ipswich. Thence they removed to a less attractive mansion, Boulge, near Woodbridge, in the same county, close to the place of his birth, and there FitzGerald resided until 1853. He then went to Farlingay Hall, an old farmhouse, where Carlyle visited him; in 1860 he moved to lodgings in Woodbridge, and in 1873 to Little Grange, where he remained until his death. Nor, at first, did he give promise of being more than an admirer, a contemplator, even in the fairy world of literature. We get charming glimpses of his sympathetic nature in some of the early letters. On the 7th of December, 1832, he says:

"The news of this week is that Thackeray has come but is going to leave again for Devonshire directly. He came very opportunely to divert my Blue Devils: notwithstanding, we do not see very much of each other: and he has now so many friends (especially the Bullers) that he has no such wish for my society. He is as full of good humour and kindness as ever. The next news is that a new volume of Tennyson is out, containing nothing more than you have in MS. except one or two things not worth having. . . . .

"I have been poring over Wordsworth lately, which has had much effect in bettering my Blue Devils: for his philosophy does not abjure melancholy, but puts a pleasant countenance upon it, and connects it with humanity. It is very well, if the sensibility that makes us fearful of ourselves is diverted to become a cause of

sympathy and interest with nature and mankind : and
this I think Wordsworth tends to do. I think I told
you of Shakespeare's sonnets before : I cannot tell you
what sweetness I find in them.

> *So by Shakespeare's sonnets roasted, and Wordsworth's poems
>   basted,*
> *My heart will be well toasted, and excellently tasted.*

"This beautiful couplet must delight you, I think."

In June, 1834, Thackeray was illustrating "my
Undine" (possibly a translation of Fouqué's romance)
"in about fourteen little coloured drawings, very nicely."
What has become of this treasure? In May, 1835,
some of the friends were together in the Lakes, and we
get, incidentally, a pleasant glimpse of the most illustrious of them :

"Alfred Tennyson stayed with me at Ambleside.
Spedding was forced to go home, till the last two days
of my stay here. I will say no more of Tennyson than
that the more I have seen of him, the more cause I have
to think him great. His little humours and grumpinesses were so droll, that I was always laughing; and
was often put in mind (strange to say) of my little unknown friend, Undine—I must, however, say, further,
that I felt what Charles Lamb describes, a sense of depression at times from the overshadowing of a so much
more lofty intellect than my own : this (though it may
seem vain to say so) I never experienced before, though
I have often been with much greater intellects : but I
could not be mistaken in the universality of his mind;

and perhaps I have received some benefit in the now more distinct consciousness of my dwarfishness."

His time, when the roses were not being pruned, and when he was not making discreet journeys in uneventful directions, was divided between music, which greatly occupied his younger thought, and literature, which slowly, but more and more exclusively, engaged his attention. His loneliness, and the high standard by which in his remote seclusion he measured all contemporary publications, gives an interest to his expressions with regard to new books, an interest which centres around himself more, perhaps, than around the work criticised. For instance, he says, in April, 1838, to the Quaker poet, Bernard Barton, who was his neighbour at Woodbridge, and whose daughter he eventually married.

"I am very heavy indeed with a kind of influenza, which has blocked up most of my senses, and put a wet blanket over my brains. This state of head has not been improved by trying to get through a new book much in fashion—Carlyle's *French Revolution*—written in a German style. An Englishman writes of French Revolutions in a German style! People say the book is very deep; but it appears to me that the meaning *seems* deep from lying under mystical language. There is no repose, nor equable movement in it: all cut up into short sentences half reflective, half narrative; so that one labours through it as vessels do through what is called a short sea—small, contrary-going waves caused by shallows, and straits, and meeting tides, &c. I like to sail before the wind over the surface of an even-rolling eloquence, like that of Bacon or the Opium-Eater. There is also pleasant fresh-water sailing with such writers as Addison. Is there any *pond*-sailing in literature? that is, drowsy, slow, and of small compass? Perhaps we may say, some Sermons. But this is only conjecture. Certainly Jeremy Taylor rolls along as majestically as any of them. We have had Alfred Tennyson here, very droll and very wayward, and much sitting up of nights till two and three in the morning, with pipes in our mouths : at which good hour we would get Alfred to give us some of his magic music, which he does between growling and smoking, and so to bed."

Few poets have been able to prepare for their life's work by so long and so dreary a novitiate. In 1839 FitzGerald gives Bernard Barton a more than commonly full account of his daily life. He goes with a fellow-fisherman, "my piscator," two miles off to fish, and has tea in a pothouse, and so walks home. "For all which idle ease," he says, "I think I must be damned." Or else upon glorious sunshiny days he lies at full length in his garden reading Tacitus, with the nightingale singing and some red anemones flaunting themselves in the sun. "A funny mixture all this; Nero, and the delicacy of spring; all very human, however. Then, at half-past one, lunch on Cambridge cream cheese; then a ride over hill and dale : then spudding up some weeds from the grass; and then, coming in, I sit down to write to you." No wonder that Carlyle, groaning in London under the weight of his work and his indigestion, would gird playfully at the "peaceable man" at Woodbridge, with his "innocent *far niente* life." FitzGerald on his part, was by no means blind to the seamy side of the loud Carlylean existence, but wished it were calmer, and retired to his Horace Walpole and his *Tale of a Tub* with fresh gusto after being tossed, as he called it, on Carlyle's "canvas waves." After an unusual burst of Chelsea eloquence, FitzGerald proposes a retreat; "We will all sit under the calm shadow of Spedding's forehead." Carlyle, meanwhile, after growing better acquainted with FitzGerald, to whom Thackeray had first presented him, became even more attached to him, and visiting him, they scraped for human bones together in the Naseby battle-field. Here is a scrap from a letter of Carlyle to FitzGerald, dated October 16, 1844:

"One day we had Alfred Tennyson here; an unforgettable day. He stayed with us till late; forgot his stick: we dismissed him with *Macpherson's Farewell.* Macpherson (see Burns) was a Highland robber; he played that Tune, of his own composition, on his way to the gallows; asked, 'If in all that crowd the Macpherson had any clansman?' holding up the fiddle that he might bequeath it to some one. 'Any kinsman, any soul that wished him well?' Nothing answered, nothing durst answer. He crushed the fiddle under his foot, and sprang off. The Tune is rough as hemp, but strong as a lion. I never hear it without something of emotion —poor Macpherson; though the artist hates to play it. Alfred's dark face grew darker, and I saw his lip slightly quivering!"

The life that slipped away at Woodbridge in a reverie so graceful and so roseate was not undisturbed from time to time by voices from the outer world calling it to action; but through a long series of years the appeal was resolutely put by. When almost all his friends were writers it could not be but that FitzGerald was conscious of a tendency to write, and there are signs in his correspondence of an occasional yielding to the tendency. But in all these early years he was never harassed by what he describes as "the strong inward call, the cruel-sweet pangs of parturition," which he observed with the curiosity of a physician, in the spirits of Tennyson and Thackeray. He knew very well that he had the power, if he chose, to pour out volume after volume, like others of the mob of gentlemen who write with ease; but his belief was that, "unless a man can do better, he had best not do at all." It is in 1847 that we find him, as a lucky discovery of Mr. Aldis Wright's informs us, plunging for the first time, though with the cryptic anonymity which he would continue to observe, into print. When Singer published his edition of Selden's *Table Talk* in that year, the illustrative matter was contributed by a gentleman whom the editor was not permitted to name. Mr. Aldis Wright has found the originals of these notes in FitzGerald's handwriting. Two years later he set his initials at the foot of a desultory memoir of Bernard Barton, prefixed to the subscription edition of the collected poems of that mild and ineffectual bard, who had died in the preceding February. It is remarkable, however, that FitzGerald's first serious enterprise in authorship was undertaken so late as in his forty-third year—at an age, that is to say, when most men who are to be famous in letters have already given copious evidence of their powers.

FitzGerald's first book, *Euphranor*, was published by Pickering in 1851, a modest little volume not passing much beyond the limits of a pamphlet. It seems to have been the child of memories of Cambridge impregnated by the Socratic talk of Spedding, who had lately been visiting FitzGerald. It is a Platonic dialogue, easily cast—somewhat in the manner, one may say, of Berkeley's *Alciphron*—in a framework of landscape, Cambridge courts and halls, the river, the locks, the deep breeze blowing through the mays and the laburnums. The characters discuss the *Godefridus* of Sir Kenelm Digby, and how the principles of chivalry can be wholesomely maintained in modern life. Slight, perhaps, and notably unambitious, *Euphranor* could scarcely have been written by any one but FitzGerald —unless, possibly, in certain moods, by Landor—and it remains the most complete and sustained of his prose works. He had scarcely published it, and, as shyly as Sabrina herself, had peeped from "the rushy-fringèd bank" of Deben to see how the world received it, before he found himself engaged on another little anonymous volume. The tiny green* 1852 quarto of *Polonius* lies before me at this moment, a presentation

---

* The grass-green cover of the original edition reminds us that "la Verdad es siémpre verde."

copy to the author's sister, "Andalusia De Soyres, from her Affecte. E. F. G." It is a collection of wise saws and modern instances, some of them his own, most of them borrowed from Bacon, Selden, Kenelm Digby, and, of the living, Carlyle and Newman, the whole graced by a charming and most characteristic preface by FitzGerald himself. And now he began with zeal to undertake the proper labour of his lifetime—he became a translator of poetry.

Six or seven years before this time, FitzGerald was corresponding on familiar terms with a younger friend, who survives him, and who appears to have been, to a very singular degree, and in the full Shakespearean sense, the "only begetter" of these ensuing translations. This was Mr. E. B. Cowell, now Professor of Sanskrit at Cambridge. As early as 1846 Mr. Cowell had introduced FitzGerald to Hafiz; in 1852 we find that the latter has "begun again to read Calderon with Cowell;" and from a letter written long afterwards to the late Sir Frederick Pollock, we learn that their first study of Calderon dated from at least 1850. Fitz-Gerald cared for but little in Spanish literature. He tried some of the other dramatists—Tirso de Molina, Lopé de Vega, Moratin, but he could take but scant interest in these. His admiration of Calderon, on the other hand, was inexhaustible, and he began to work assiduously at the task of translating him, taking all Shelley's pleasure in the "starry autos." The volume called *Six Dramas of Calderon, freely translated by Edward FitzGerald*, was issued by Pickering in 1853, and is the only one of all FitzGerald's publications which bears his name upon it. The six plays are: *The Painter of his own Dishonour, Keep your own Secret, Gil Perez the Gallician, Three Judgments at a Blow, The Mayor of Zalanca,* and *Beware of Smooth Water.* The book is now of extreme scarcity, the translator having withdrawn it from circulation in one of his singular fits of caprice, partly, I believe, on account of the severity with which its freedom as a paraphrase was attacked. I am bound to say, however, that I find no traces of irritation on this subject in his letters of 1853, which refer to various reviews in a very moderate and sensible spirit.

The *Calderon* had scarcely passed through the printer's hands when FitzGerald took up the study of Persian, still in company with and under the direction of Mr. Cowell. In 1854, when he was visiting that friend at Oxford, he began to try his hand on a verse translation of the *Salámán and Absál* of Jámí, "whose ingenious prattle I am stilting into too Miltonic verse." This was published in 1856, anonymously, with a picturesque "Life of Jámi," and a curious frontispiece of warriors playing polo. Meanwhile Mr. Cowell was appointed Professor of History at a Calcutta college, and one main stimulus to steady production was removed out of FitzGerald's life. Yet, by good fortune for us, Mr. Cowell's absence from England induced FitzGerald to write to him more fully about his work than he would have done if the friends could have met. And here, on the 20th of March, 1857, we are allowed to be present at the first conception of what was afterwards to become the famous and admired *Omar Khayyám*:

"To-day I have been writing twenty pages of a metrical Sketch of the Mantic, for such uses as I told you of. It is an amusement to me to take what liberties I like with these Persians, who (as I think) are not poets enough to frighten one from such excursions, and who really do want a little art to shape them. I don't speak of Jeláleddín whom I know so little of (enough to show me that he is no great artist, however), nor of Hafiz, whose *best* is untranslatable because he is the best musician of words. Old Johnson said the poets were the best preservers of a language: for people must go to the original to relish them. I am sure that what Tennyson said to you is true: that Hafiz is the most Eastern—or, he should have said, most *Persian*—of the Persians. He is the best representative of their character, whether his Sáki and wine be real or mystical. Their religion and philosophy is soon seen through, and always seems to me *cuckooed* over like a borrowed thing, which people, once having got, don't know how to parade enough. To be sure, their roses and nightingales are repeated enough; but Hafiz and old Omar Khayyám ring like true metal. The philosophy of the latter is, alas! one that never fails in the world."

He was soon keenly engaged on his task; had in April opened up a correspondence with Garcin de Tassy about texts of Omar in the Paris libraries.

This was the busiest year of FitzGerald's literary life. In May he was already beginning to warn his friend of another possible "sudden volume of translations," the desire to conquer a province of Æschylus in his peculiar way having seized him. The only result, however, was the preparation—but at what date I do not seem able to discover—of that extraordinary translation of the *Agamemnon*, eventually printed without name of author, title-page, or imprint, in a hideous cover of grocer's azure, which is one of the rarest of FitzGerald's issues. In January, 1858, he began the dismal business of trying, and at first vainly trying, to find a publisher bold enough to embark on the perilous enterprise of printing the little pamphlet of immortal music called *The Rubáiyát of Omar Khayyám*. On the subject of this publication much has been loosely said and conjecturally reported of late years. We may, therefore, be glad to read FitzGerald's own account, in a letter to the late Master of Trinity:

"As to my own peccadilloes in verse, which never pretend to be original, this is the story of *Rubáiyát*. I had translated them partly for Cowell: young Parker asked me some years ago for something for Fraser, and I gave him the less wicked of these to use if he chose. He kept them for two years without using: and as I saw he didn't want them I printed some copies with Quaritch; and, keeping some for myself, gave him the rest. Cowell, to whom I sent a copy, was naturally alarmed at it; he being a very religious man: nor have I given any other copy but to George Borrow, to whom

I had once lent the Persian, and to old Donne when he was down here the other day, to whom I was showing a passage in another book which brought my old Omar up."

On the 15th of January, 1859, as Mr. W. Aldis Wright has been kind enough to ascertain for me, the *Rubáiyát* was issued, in the casual way above indicated, and fell absolutely flat upon the market. There is no evidence in FitzGerald's correspondence that it attracted the smallest attention, and, except for a letter from Mr. Ruskin, which circled the globe for ten years (this sounds incredibly characteristic, but seems to be true) before it reached its address, the first publication of his magnificent poem appears to have brought FitzGerald no breath of recognition from the world outside the circle of his friends. The copies in Mr. Quaritch's shop seem to have found no buyers, and to have gravitated rather surprisingly soon to the fourpenny boxes outside the booksellers' stalls. Here Dante Gabriel Rossetti, so legend relates, discovered the hid treasure in 1860, and proclaimed it among his friends, Mr. Swinburne being forward in the generous race to make the poem appreciated at its proper value. It marks a rise in the barometer of popularity that Monckton Milnes (Lord Houghton) is anxiously inquiring for a copy or two in May, 1861. Yet it was not until 1868 that a second edition, now scarcely less rare and no whit less interesting to the collector, was called for. Since that time, much revised by its far too careful author, the *Rubáiyát of Omar Khayyám* has been reprinted in all manner of shapes, both on this side of the Atlantic and on the other. To pursue the record of his literary life, Fitzgerald translated two more plays of Calderon, the *Magico prodigioso*, at which Shelley had tried his hand, and the *Vida es Sueño*, which Trench had attempted. These he never published, but in 1865 he printed them, without title-page, and sent the strange little volume, in a grey paper wrapper, to a few of his friends. With the exception of the two *Œdipus* dramas, circulated in the same quaint, shy way, in 1880, these were the last of Fitzgerald's poetical translations.

He had grown more and more interested in the water-way leading from the pastoral meadows of Woodbridge to the sea, the salt road between the trees called Bawdsey Haven, which brings you, if you go far enough down it, to the German Ocean at last. His favourite companions became fishermen and the captains of boats, and in 1867 an old wish was realised at length, when FitzGerald became part owner of a herring-lugger—*The Meum and Tuum* as he called her, and possessed a captain of his own. Later on, he bought a yacht, *The Scandal*. "Nothing but ship," he says, from June to November, through all those months, "not having lain, I believe, for three consecutive nights in Christian sheets," but mostly knocking about somewhere outside of Lowestoft. The theory was that the lugger should pay her way, but FitzGerald and his captain, "a grand, tender soul, lodged in a suitable carcase," did not make the profit that they hoped for, and after four years of considerable anxiety, FitzGerald parted from his boat and from her master.

The latter was a humble friend in whom, physically and spiritually, there must have been something splendidly attractive, and regarding whom FitzGerald uses phraseology otherwise reserved for Tennyson and Thackeray. The poet still kept a boat upon the Deben, but went out no more upon the deep after herrings and mackerel, in company with his auburn-haired and blue-eyed giant from Lowestoft, "altogether," he says, "the greatest man I have known."

And so, almost imperceptibly, as the reader moves down the series of these delightful letters, he finds that the writer, in his delicate epicureanism, is, without repining at it, growing old. A selection from his early favourite poet, a Suffolk man like himself, George Crabbe, is his last literary enterprise, and so on the 14th of June, 1883, in his seventy-fifth year, he rather suddenly passes away painlessly in his sleep. His own words shall be his epitaph: "An idle fellow, but one whose friendships were more like loves."

The strange issues of Calderon, of Æschylus, of Jámí, of Sophocles, with which it was FitzGerald's pleasure to confound bibliographers, are now great rarities; not one of all his printed works, except the *Omar Khayyám*, has hitherto been easy to obtain. We may generally say in looking over all these versions, that FitzGerald more than any other recent translator of poetry, carried out that admirable rule of Sir John Denham's, that the translator's business is not "alone to translate language into language, but poesie into poesie; and poesie is of so subtle a spirit, that in pouring out of one language into another, it will all evaporate, if a new spirit be not added in the translation." FitzGerald's versions are so free, he is so little bound by the details of his orignal, he is so indifferent to the timid pedantry of the ordinary writer who empties verse out of the cup of one language into that of another, that we may attempt with him what would be a futile task with almost every other English translator—we may estimate from his versions alone what manner of poet he was.

In attempting to form such an estimate we are bound to recognise that his best-known work is also his best. The *Omar Khayyám* of FitzGerald takes its place in the third period of Victorian poetry, as an original force wholly in sympathy with other forces of which its author took no personal cognisance. Whether or no it accurately represents the sentiments of a Persian astronomer of the eleventh century is a question which fades into insignificance beside the fact that it stimulated and delighted a generation of young readers, to whom it appealed in the same manner, and along parallel lines with, the poetry of Morris, Swinburne, and the Rossettis. After the lapse of thirty years we are able to perceive that in the series of poetical publications of capital importance which marked the close of the fifties it takes its natural place. In 1858 appeared *The Defence of Guinevere;* in 1859, the *Rubáiyát of Omar Khayyám;* in 1860, *The Queen-Mother and Rosamond;* in 1862, *Goblin Market;* while, although the *Poems* of D. G. Rossetti did not finally see the light till 1870, his presence, his spiritual influence, had animated the group. That FitzGerald was ignorant of, or wholly indifferent to, the existence of these his compeers did not affect his relationship to them, nor their natural and instinctive recognition of his imaginative kinship to themselves. The same reassertion of the sensuous elements of literature, the same obedience to the call for a richer music and a more exotic and impassioned aspect of manners, the same determination to face the melancholy problems of life and find a solace for them in art, were to be found in the anonymous pamphlet of Oriental reverie as in the romances, dramas, songs, and sonnets of the four younger friends.

So much more interesting to us, if we will look sensibly at the matter, is FitzGerald than the Omar Khayyám whose mantle he chose to masquerade in that we are not vexed but delighted to learn from Mr. Aldis Wright that the opening stanza, which ran thus in the edition of 1859:

> *Awake! for morning in the bowl of night*
> *Has flung the stone that puts the stars to flight;*
> *And lo! the hunter of the East has caught*
> *The Sultan's turret in a noose of light,*

is wholly his own, and represents nothing in the original. It was judged by his earliest critics to be too close a following of the fantastic allusiveness of the Persian, and the poet—surely with his tongue set in his cheek—modified his own invention to the smoother but less spirited:

*Wake ! for the sun behind yon Eastern height
Has chased the session of the stars from night ;
   And, to the field of heav'n ascending, strikes
The Sultan's turret with a shaft of light.*

It is well to remind ourselves of these two versions, of which each is good, though the first be best, because FitzGerald was sufficiently ill-advised to exchange for both a much tamer version, which now holds its place in the text. These alterations, however, are very significant to the critic, and exhibit the extreme care with which FitzGerald revised and re-revised his work.

To judge, however, of his manner as a translator, or rather as a paraphraser, we must examine not merely the most famous and remarkable of his writings, but his treatment of Spanish and Greek drama, and of the narrative of Jámí. It appears that he took Dryden's licence, and carried it further ; that he steeped himself in the language and feeling of his author, and then threw over his version the robe of his own peculiar style. Every great translator does this to some extent, and we do not recognise in Chapman's breathless gallop the staid and polished Homer that marches down the couplets of Pope. But then, both Pope and Chapman had, in the course of abundant original composition, made themselves each the possessor of a style which he threw without difficulty around the shoulders of his paraphrase. In the unique case of FitzGerald— since Fairfax can scarcely be considered in the same category—a poet of no marked individuality in his purely independent verse created for himself, in the act of approaching masterpieces of widely different race and age, a poetical style so completely his own that we recognise it at sight as his. The normal instances of this manner are familiar to us in *Omar Khayyám*. They are characterised by a melody which has neither the variety of Tennyson nor the vehemence of Mr. Swinburne, neither the motion of a river nor of the sea, but which rather reminds us, in its fulness and serenity, of the placid motion of the surface of a lake, or of his own grassy estuary of the Deben; and finally by a voluptuous and novel use of the commonplaces of poetry—the rose, the vine, the nightingale, the moon. There are examples of this typical manner of FitzGerald to be found in *Omar Khayyám*, which are unsurpassed for their pure qualities as poetry, and which must remain always characteristic of what was best in a certain class of Victorian verse. Such are:

> *Alas, that spring should vanish with the rose!*
> *That youth's sweet-scented manuscript should close;*
>   *The nightingale that in the branches sang,*
> *Ah, whence and whither flown again, who knows!*

and (a gem spoiled in recutting, after the first edition, by the capricious jeweller):

> *Thus with a loaf of bread beneath the bough,*
> *A flask of wine, a book of verse—and thou*
>   *Beside me singing in the wilderness—*
> *And wilderness is Paradise enow.*

Nothing quite so good, perhaps, as these and many more which might be quoted from the *Omar Khayyám*, is to be found in the other translations, yet wherever the latter are happiest they betray the same hand and murmur the same accents. It is in *The Mighty Magician* that we meet with such characteristic stanzas as this:

> *Who that in his hour of glory*
>   *Walks the kingdom of the rose,*
> *And misapprehends the story*
>   *Which through all the garden blows;*
> *Which the southern air who brings*
> *It touches, and the leafy strings*
>   *Lightly to the touch respond;*
> *And nightingale to nightingale*
>   *Answering on bough beyond—*
> *Nightingale to nightingale*
>   *Answering on bough beyond.*

While the following passage, perhaps the richest and most memorable in FitzGerald's minor writings, is found in the *Salámán and Absál:*

> *When they had sail'd their vessel for a moon,*
> *And marr'd their beauty with the wind o' the sea,*
> *Suddenly in mid-sea reveal'd itself*
> *An isle, beyond imagination fair;*
> *An isle that was all garden; not a flower,*
> *Nor bird of plumage like the flower, but there;*
> *Some like the flower, and others like the leaf;*
> *Some, as the pheasant and the dove, adorn'd*

With crown and collar, over whom, alone,
The jewell'd peacock like a sultan shone :
While the musicians, and among them chief
The nightingale, sang hidden in the trees,
Which, arm in arm, from fingers quivering
With any breath of air, fruit of all kind
Down scatter'd in profusion to their feet,
Where fountains of sweet water ran between,
And sun and shadow chequer-chased the green,
This Iram-garden seem'd in secrecy
Blowing the rosebud of its revelation;
Or Paradise, forgetful of the dawn
Of Audit, lifted from her face the veil.

In reading these sumptuous verses the reader may be inclined to wonder why *Salámán and Absál* is not as widely known and as universally admired as the *Omar Khayyám*. If it were constantly sustained at anything like this level it would be so admired and known, but it is, unfortunately, both crabbed and unequal.

It was in 1854, as FitzGerald reminds Professor Cowell in a very interesting letter, that these friends began to read Jámí together. We have seen that it was not until 1856 and after the completion of the *Salámán and Absál* that the same friend placed Omar in FitzGerald's hands. The paraphrase of Jámí, therefore, is the earlier of the two, and represents the style of the English poet at a stage when it was still unfinished and, I think, imperfectly refined. The narrative of Jámí is diffuse, and, as FitzGerald soon found, "not line by line precious;" he was puzzled how to retain his character and yet not permit it to be tedious, and he has not wholly succeeded in clearing his poem from the second horn of the dilemma. The original text of 1856 differs in almost every line, and sometimes essentially, from that now published in FitzGerald's work. I do not know on what the later text is founded, but probably on a revision found among his papers. I confess that the bolder early version seems to me considerably the more poetical. *Sálámán and Absál* consists of a mystical preliminary invocation, in which the problem of responsibility and free-will, in the form which interested the English poet so much, is boldly stated and the double question put:

> *If I—this spirit that inspires me whence?*
> *If thou—then what this sensual impotence?*

and of the story, told in three parts, with a moral or transcendental summing-up at the close. The metrical form chosen for the main narrative is blank verse, with occasional lapses into rhyme. These, in all probability, respond to some peculiarity in the Persian original, but they are foreign to the genius of English prosody, and they produce an effect of poverty upon the ear, which is alternately tempted and disappointed. There are, moreover, incessant interludes or episodical interpolations, which are treated in an ambling measure of four beats, something like the metre of *Hiawatha*, but again with occasional and annoying introductions of rhyme. It is obvious, at the outset, that we do not see FitzGerald here exercising that perfect instinct for form which he afterwards developed; he was trammelled, no doubt, by his desire to repeat the effects he discovered in the Persian, and had not yet asserted his own genius in what Dryden called metaphrase. Nevertheless, *Salámán and Absál* contains passages of great beauty, such as that in which the poet, in wayward dejection, confesses that his worn harp is no longer modulated, and that

> *Methinks*
> *'Twere time to break and cast it in the fire:*
> *The vain old harp, that, breathing from its strings*
> *No music more to charm the ears of man,*
> *May, from its scented ashes, as it burns,*
> *Breathe resignation to the harper's soul.*

And the description of Absál, the lovely infant nurse of the new-born Salámán (1856 text):

> *Her years not twenty, from the silver line,*
> *Dividing the musk-harvest of her hair,*
> *Down to her foot, that trampled crowns of kings,*
> *A moon of beauty full.*

Very curious and charming, too, are the descriptions of Salámán's victory over the princes at polo, and his headlong ride to the shore of the abyss that was haunted by the starry dragon, and whose island crags cut its surface "as silver scissors slice a blue brocade."

A third Persian poem, the *Bird-Parliament* of Faríd-

Uddín Attar, written immediately after the publication of *Omar Khayyám* in 1859, was first printed by Mr. Aldis Wright thirty years later, and forms a very important addition to FitzGerald's works. It is a long, mystical piece of Oriental transcendentalism, the best part of which is the opening pages, in which the various birds are introduced, spreading their jewelled plumage one by one before the tajidar, the royal lapwing, who is their shah or sultan. When the poem becomes purely philosophical, it seems to me to become less attractive, perhaps sometimes a little tedious; yet the versification is always charming, the heroic couplet treated as smoothly and correctly as by Congreve or Addison, but with far greater richness.

Of FitzGerald as a prose writer there has hitherto been little known. His correspondence now reveals him, unless I am much mistaken, as one of the most pungent, individual, and picturesque of English letter-writers. Rarely do we discover a temperament so mobile under a surface so serene and sedentary; rarely so feminine a sensibility side by side with so virile an intelligence. He is moved by every breath of Nature; every change of hue in earth or air affects him; and all these are reflected, as in a camera obscura, in the richly-coloured moving mirror of his letters. It will not surprise one reader of this correspondence if the name of its author should grow to be set, in common parlance, beside those of Gray and Cowper for the fidelity and humanity of his addresses to his private friends. Meanwhile, we ought, perhaps, to have remem-

Edward FitzGerald

bered what beautiful pages there were in *Euphranor*, and in particular to have recalled that passage about the University boat-races which Lord Tennyson, no easy critic to satisfy, has pronounced to be one of the most beautiful fragments of English prose extant. Not many in this generation have met with *Euphranor*, and I may quote this passage with the certainty that it is new to all or nearly all of my readers :

"Townsmen and gownsmen, with the tassell'd Fellow-commoner sprinkled here and there—reading men and sporting men—Fellows, and even Masters of Colleges, not indifferent to the prowess of their respective crews—all these, conversing on all sorts of topics, from the slang in *Bell's Life* to the last new German revelation, and moving in ever-changing groups down the shore of the river, at whose farther bend was a little knot of ladies gathered up on a green knoll faced and illuminated by the beams of the setting sun. Beyond which point was at length heard some indistinct shouting, which gradually increased, until 'They are off—they are coming!' suspended other conversation among ourselves; and suddenly the head of the first boat turned the corner; and then another close upon it; and then a third; the crews pulling with all their might compacted into perfect rhythm; and the crowd on shore turning round to follow along with them, waving hats and caps, and cheering, 'Bravo, St. John's!' 'Go it, Trinity!'—the high crest and blowing forelock of Phidippus's mare, and he himself shouting encouragement to his crew, conspicuous over all—until, the boats reaching us, we also were caught up in the returning tide of spectators, and hurried back toward the goal; where we arrived just in time to see the ensign of Trinity lowered from its pride of place, and the eagle of St John's soaring there instead. Then, waiting a little while to hear how the winner had won, and the loser lost, and watching Phidippus engaged in eager conversation with his defeated brethren, I took Euphranor and Lexilogus under either arm (Lycion having got into better company elsewhere) and walked home with them across the meadow leading to the town, whither the dusky troops of gownsmen with all their confused voices seemed as it were evaporating in the twilight, while a nightingale began to be heard among the flowering chestnuts of Jesus."

Who is rashly to decide what place may not finally be awarded to a man capable of such admirable feats in English prose and verse? There can be little doubt that when much contemporary clamour has died out for ever, the clear note of the Nightingale of Woodbridge will still be heard from the alleys of his Persian garden.

1889.

# WALT WHITMAN

Walt Whitman

I

FATIMA was permitted, nay encouraged, to make use of all the rooms, so elegantly and commodiously furnished, in Bluebeard Castle, with one exception. It was in vain that the housemaid and the cook pointed out to her that each of the ladies who had preceded her as a tenant had smuggled herself into that one forbidden chamber and had never come out again. Their sad experience was thrown away upon Fatima, who penetrated the fatal apartment and became an object of melancholy derision. The little room called "Walt Whitman," in the castle of literature, reminds one of that in which the relics of Bluebeard's levity were stored. We all know that discomfort and perplexity await us there, that nobody ever came back from it with an intelligible message, that it is piled with the bones of critics; yet such is the perversity of the analytic mind, that each one of us, sooner or later, finds himself peeping through the keyhole and fumbling at the lock.

As the latest of these imprudent explorers, I stand a moment with the handle in my hand and essay a defence of those whose skeletons will presently be discovered. Was it their fault? Was their failure not rather due to a sort of magic that hangs over the place? To drop metaphor, I am sadly conscious that, after reading what a great many people of authority and of assumption have written about Whitman—reading it, too, in a humble spirit—though I have been stimulated and entertained, I have not been at all instructed. Pleasant light, of course, has been thrown on the critics themselves and on their various peculiarities. But upon Whitman, upon the place he holds in literature and life, upon the questions, what he was and why he was, surely very little. To me, at least, after all the oceans of talk, after all the extravagant eulogy, all the mad vituperation, he remains perfectly cryptic and opaque. I find no reason given by these authorities why he should have made his appearance, or what his appearance signifies. I am told that he is abysmal, putrid, glorious, universal and contemptible. I like these excellent adjectives, but I cannot see how to apply them to Whitman. Yet, like a boy at a shooting-gallery, I cannot go home till I, too, have had my six shots at this running-deer.

On the main divisions of literature it seems that a critic should have not merely a firm opinion, but sound argument to back that opinion. It is a pilgarlicky mind that is satisfied with saying, "I like you, Dr. Fell, the reason why I cannot tell." Analysis is the art of telling the reason why. But still more feeble and slovenly is the criticism that has to say, "I liked Dr. Fell yesterday and I don't like him to-day, but I can give no reason." The shrine of Walt Whitman, however, is strewn around with remarks of this kind. Poor Mr.

Walt Whitman

Swinburne has been cruelly laughed at for calling him a "strong-winged soul, with prophetic lips hot with the blood-beats of song," and yet a drunken apple-woman reeling in a gutter. But he is not alone in this inconsistency. Almost every competent writer who has attempted to give an estimate of Whitman has tumbled about in the same extraordinary way. Something mephitic breathes from this strange personality, something that maddens the judgment until the wisest lose their self-control.

Therefore, I propound a theory. It is this, that there is no real Walt Whitman, that is to say, that he cannot be taken as any other figure in literature is taken, as an entity of positive value and defined characteristics, as, for instance, we take the life and writings of Racine, or of Keats, or of Jeremy Taylor, including the style with the substance, the teaching with the idiosyncrasy. In these ordinary cases the worth and specific weight of the man are not greatly affected by our attitude towards him. An atheist or a quaker may contemplate the writings of the Bishop of Down without sympathy; that does not prevent the *Holy Dying* from presenting, even to the mind of such an opponent, certain defined features which are unmodified by like or dislike. This is true of any fresh or vivid talent which may have appeared among us yesterday. But I contend that it is not true of Whitman. Whitman is mere *bathybius;* he is literature in the condition of protoplasm—an intellectual organism so simple that it takes the instant impression of whatever mood approaches it. Hence the critic who touches Whitman is immediately confronted with his own image stamped upon that viscid and tenacious surface. He finds, not what Whitman has to give, but what he himself has brought. And when, in quite another mood, he comes again to Whitman, he finds that other self of his own stamped upon the provoking protoplasm.

If this theory is allowed a moment's consideration, it cannot, I think, but tend to be accepted. It accounts for all the difficulties in the criticism of Whitman. It shows us why Robert Louis Stevenson has found a Stevenson in *Leaves of Grass*, and John Addington Symonds a Symonds. It explains why Emerson considered the book "the most extraordinary piece of wit and wisdom that America has yet [in 1855] produced;" why Thoreau thought all the sermons ever preached not equal to it for divinity; why Italian *dilettanti* and Scandinavian gymnasts, anarchists and parsons and champions of women's rights, the most opposite and incongruous types, have the habit of taking Whitman to their hearts for a little while and then flinging him away from them in abhorrence, and, perhaps, of drawing him to them again with passion. This last, however, I think occurs more rarely. Almost every sensitive and natural person has gone through a period of fierce Whitmanomania; but it is a disease which rarely afflicts the same patient more than once. It is, in fact, a sort of highly-irritated egotism come to a head, and people are almost always better after it.

Unless we adopt some such theory as this, it is

difficult to account in any way for the persistent influence of Walt Whitman's writings. They have now lasted about forty years, and show no sign whatever of losing their vitality. Nobody is able to analyse their charm, yet the charm is undeniable. They present no salient features, such as have been observed in all other literature, from Homer and David down to the latest generation. They offer a sort of Plymouth Brethrenism of form, a negation of all the laws and ritual of literature. As a book, to be a living book, must contain a vigorous and appropriate arrangement of words, this one solitary feature occurs in *Leaves of Grass*. I think it is not to be denied by any candid critic, however inimical, that passages of extreme verbal felicity are to be found frequently scattered over the pages of Whitman's rhapsodies. But, this one concession made to form, there is no other. Not merely are rhythm and metre conspicuously absent, but composition, evolution, vertebration of style, even syntax and the limits of the English tongue, are disregarded. Every reader who comes to Whitman starts upon an expedition to the virgin forest. He must take his conveniences with him. He will make of the excursion what his own spirit dictates. There are solitudes, fresh air, rough landscape, and a well of water, but if he wishes to enjoy the latter he must bring his own cup with him. When people are still young and like roughing it, they appreciate a picnic into Whitman-land, but it is not meant for those who choose to see their intellectual comforts round them.

II

In the early and middle years of his life, Whitman was obscure and rarely visited. When he grew old, pilgrims not unfrequently took scrip and staff, and set out to worship him. Several accounts of his appearance and mode of address on these occasions have been published, and if I add one more it must be my excuse that the visit to be described was not undertaken in the customary spirit. All other accounts, so far as I know, of interviews with Whitman have been written by disciples who approached the shrine adoring and ready to be dazzled. The visitor whose experience— and it was a very delightful one—is now to be chronicled, started under what was, perhaps, the disadvantage of being very unwilling to go; at least, it will be admitted that the tribute—for tribute it has to be—is all the more sincere.

When I was in Boston, in the winter of 1884, I received a note from Whitman asking me not to leave America without coming to see him. My first instinct was promptly to decline the invitation. Camden, New Jersey, was a very long way off. But better counsels prevailed; curiosity and civility combined to draw me, and I wrote to him that I would come. It would be fatuous to mention all this, if it were not that I particularly wish to bring out the peculiar magic of the old man, acting, not on a disciple, but on a stiff-necked and froward unbeliever.

To reach Camden, one must arrive at Philadelphia,

where I put up on the 2nd of January, 1885, ready to pass over into New Jersey next morning. I took the hall-porter of the hotel into my confidence, and asked if he had ever heard of Mr. Whitman. Oh, yes, they all knew "Walt," he said; on fine days he used to cross over on the ferry and take the tram into Philadelphia. He liked to stroll about in Chestnut Street and look at the people, and if you smiled at him he would smile back again; everybody knew "Walt." In the North, I had been told that he was almost bedridden, in consequence of an attack of paralysis. This seemed inconsistent with wandering round Philadelphia.

The distance being considerable, I started early on the 3rd, crossed the broad Delaware River, where blocks of ice bumped and crackled around us, and saw the flat shores of New Jersey expanding in front, raked by the broad morning light. I was put ashore in a crude and apparently uninhabited village, grim with that concentrated ugliness that only an American township in the depth of winter can display. Nobody to ask the way, or next to nobody. I wandered aimlessly about, and was just ready to give all I possessed to be back again in New York, when I discovered that I was opposite No. 328 Mickle Street, and that on a minute brass plate was engraved "W. Whitman." I knocked at this dreary little two-storey tenement house, and wondered what was going to happen. A melancholy woman opened the door; it was too late now to go away. But before I could speak, a large figure, hobbling down the stairs, called out in a cheery voice, "Is that my friend?" Suddenly, by I know not what magnetic charm, all wire-drawn literary reservations faded out of being, and one's only sensation was of gratified satisfaction at being the "friend" of this very nice old gentleman.

There was a good deal of greeting on the stairs, and then the host, moving actively, though clumsily, and with a stick, advanced to his own dwelling-room on the first storey. The opening impression was, as the closing one would be, of extreme simplicity. A large room, without carpet on the scrubbed planks, a small bedstead, a little round stove with a stack-pipe in the middle of the room, one chair—that was all the furniture. On the walls and in the fireplace such a miserable wall-paper—tinted, with a spot—as one sees in the bedrooms of labourers' cottages; no pictures hung in the room, but pegs and shelves loaded with objects. Various boxes lay about, and one huge clamped trunk, and heaps, mountains of papers in a wild confusion, swept up here and there into stacks and peaks; but all the room, and the old man himself, clean in the highest degree, raised to the nth power of stainlessness, scoured and scrubbed to such a pitch that dirt seemed defied for all remaining time. Whitman, in particular, in his suit of hodden grey and shirt thrown wide open at the throat, his grey hair and whiter beard voluminously flowing, seemed positively blanched with cleanliness; the whole man sand-white with spotlessness, like a deal table that has grown old under the scrubbing-brush.

Whitman sat down in the one chair with a small poker in his hand and spent much of his leisure in feeding and irritating the stove. I cleared some papers away from off a box and sat opposite to him. When he was not actively engaged upon the stove his steady attention was fixed upon his visitor, and I had a perfect opportunity of forming a mental picture of him. He sat with a very curious pose of the head thrown backward, as if resting it one vertebra lower down the spinal column than other people do, and thus tilting his face a little upwards. With his head so poised and the whole man fixed in contemplation of the interlocutor, he seemed to pass into a state of absolute passivity, waiting for remarks or incidents, the glassy eyes half closed, the large knotted hands spread out before him. So he would remain, immovable for a quarter of an hour at a time, even the action of speech betraying no movement, the lips hidden under a cascade of beard. If it be true that all remarkable human beings resemble animals, then Walt Whitman was like a cat—a great old grey Angora Tom, alert in repose, serenely blinking under his combed waves of hair, with eyes inscrutably dreaming.

His talk was elemental, like his writings. It had none of the usual ornaments or irritants of conversation. It welled out naturally, or stopped ; it was innocent of every species of rhetoric or epigram. It was the perfectly simple utterance of unaffected urbanity. So, I imagine, an Oriental sage would talk, in a low uniform tone, without any excitement or haste, without emphasis, in a land where time and flurry were unknown. Whitman sat there with his great head tilted back, smiling serenely, and he talked about himself. He mentioned his poverty, which was patent, and his paralysis; those were the two burdens beneath which he crouched, like Issachar; he seemed to be quite at home with both of them, and scarcely heeded them. I think I asked leave to move my box, for the light began to pour in at the great uncurtained window; and then Whitman said that some one had promised him a gift of curtains, but he was not eager for them, he thought they "kept out some of the light." Light and air, that was all he wanted; and through the winter he sat there patiently waiting for the air and light of summer, when he would hobble out again and bask his body in a shallow creek he knew "back of Camden." Meanwhile he waited, waited with infinite patience, uncomplaining, thinking about the sand, and the thin hot layer of water over it, in that shy New Jersey creek. And he winked away in silence, while I thought of the Indian poet Valmiki, when, in a trance of voluptuous abstraction, he sat under the fig-tree and was slowly eaten of ants.

In the bareness of Whitman's great double room only two objects suggested art in any way, but each of these was appropriate. One was a print of a Red Indian, given him, he told me, by Catlin; it had inspired the passage about "the red aborigines" in *Starting from Paumanok*. The other—positively the sole and only thing that redeemed the bareness of the back-room where Whitman's bound works were stored—was a photograph of a very handsome young man in a boat, sculling. I asked him about this portrait and he said several notable things in consequence. He explained, first of all, that this was one of his greatest friends, a professional oarsman from Canada, a well-known sporting character. He continued, that these were the people he liked best, athletes who had a business in the open air; that those were the plainest and most affectionate of men, those who lived in the light and air and had to study to keep their bodies clean and fresh and ruddy; that his soul went out to such people, and that they were strangely drawn to him, so that at the lowest ebb of his fortunes, when the world reviled him and ridiculed him most, fortunate men of this kind, highly prosperous as gymnasts or runners, had sought him out and had been friendly to him. "And now," he went on, "I only wait for the spring, to hobble out with my staff into the woods, and when I can sit all day long close to a set of woodmen at their work, I am perfectly happy, for something of their life mixes with the smell of the chopped timber, and it passes into my veins and I am old and ill no longer." I think these were his precise words, and they struck me more than anything else that he said throughout that long and pleasant day I spent with him.

It might be supposed, and I think that even admirers have said, that Whitman had no humour. But that seemed to me not quite correct. No boisterous humour, truly, but a gentle sort of sly fun, something like

Tennyson's, he certainly showed. For example, he told me of some tribute from India, and added, with a twinkling smile, "You see, I 'sound my barbaric yawp over the roofs of the world.'" But this was rare: mostly he seemed dwelling in a vague pastoral past life, the lovely days when he was young, and went about with "the boys" in the sun. He read me many things; a new "poem," intoning the long irregular lines of it not very distinctly; and a preface to some new edition. All this has left, I confess, a dim impression, swallowed up in the serene self-unconsciousness, the sweet, dignified urbanity, the feline immobility.

As I passed from the little house and stood in dull, deserted Mickle Street once more, my heart was full of affection for this beautiful old man, who had just said in his calm accents, "Good-bye, my friend!" I felt that the experience of the day was embalmed by something that a great poet had written long ago, but I could not find what it was till we started once more to cross the frosty Delaware; then it came to me, and I knew that when Shelley spoke of

> *Peace within and calm around,*
> *And that content, surpassing wealth,*
> *The sage in meditation found,*
> *And walk'd with inward glory crown'd,*

he had been prophesying of Walt Whitman, nor shall I ever read those lines again without thinking of the old rhapsodist in his empty room, glorified by patience and philosophy.

And so an unbeliever went to see Walt Whitman, and was captivated without being converted.

III

It is related of the great Condé that, at the opening of his last campaign, sunken in melancholy, half maddened with fatigue and the dog-star heat of summer, having reached at length the cool meadows in front of the Abbey of St. Antoine, he suddenly leaped from his horse, flung away his arms and his clothing, and rolled stark-naked in the grass under a group of trees. Having taken this bath amidst his astonished officers, he rose smiling and calm, permitted himself to be dressed and armed anew, and rode to battle with all his accustomed resolution. The instinct which this anecdote illustrates lies deep down in human nature, and the more we are muffled up in social conventions the more we occasionally long for a whimsical return to nudity. If a writer is strong enough, from one cause or another, to strip the clothing off from civilisation, that writer is sure of a welcome from thousands of over-civilised readers. Now the central feature of the writings of Walt Whitman is their nakedness. In saying this I do not refer to half-a-dozen phrases, which might with ease be eliminated, that have thrown Mrs. Grundy into fits. No responsible criticism will make a man stand or fall by what are simply examples of the carrying of a theory to excess. But of the theory itself I speak, and it is one of uncompromising openness. It is a defence of bare human nature, stripped, not merely of all its trappings and badges, but even of those garments which are universally held necessary to keep the cold away. In so many of his writings, and particularly, of course, in the *Discours* of 1750, Rousseau undertook the defence of social nudity. He called upon his world, which prided itself so much upon its elegance, to divest the body politic of all its robes. He declared that while Nature has made man happy and virtuous, society it is that renders him miserable and depraved, therefore let him get rid of social conventions and roll naked in the grass under the elm-trees. The invitation, as I have said, is one which never lacks acceptance, and Rousseau was followed into the forest by a multitude.

If Walt Whitman goes further than Rousseau, it merely is that he is more elementary. The temperament of the American is in every direction less complex. He has none of the restless intellectual vivacity, none of the fire, none of the passionate hatred of iniquity which mark the French philosopher. With Walt Whitman a coarse simplicity suffices, a certain blunt and determined negation of artificiality of every kind. He is, roughly speaking, a keenly observant and sentient being, without thought, without selection, without intensity, egged on by his nervous system to a revelation of himself. He records his own sensations one after another, careful only to present them in veracious form, without drapery or rhetoric. His charm for others is precisely this, that he observes so closely, and records so great a multitude of observations, and presents them with so complete an absence of prejudice, that any person who approaches his writings with an unbiassed mind must discover in them a reflection of some part of himself. This I believe to be the secret of the extraordinary attraction which these rhapsodical utterances have for most emotional persons at one crisis or another in their life's development. But I think criticism ought to be able to distinguish between the semi-hysterical pleasure of self-recognition and the sober and legitimate delights of literature.

The works of Walt Whitman cover a great many pages, but the texture of them is anything but subtle. When once the mind perceives what it is that Whitman says, it is found that he repeats himself over and over again, and that all his "gospel" (as the odious modern cant puts it) is capable of being strained into very narrow limits. One "poem" contains at least the germ of all the sheaves and sheaves of writing that Whitman published. There is not one aspect of his nature which is not stated, or more than broadly hinted at, in the single piece which he named after himself, "Walt Whitman." It was appropriately named, for an unclothing of himself, an invitation to all the world to come and prove that, stripped of his clothes, he was exactly like everybody else, was the essence of his religion, his philosophy, and his poetry.

It is not unfair to concentrate attention on the section of sixty pages which bears the name "Walt Whitman" in the volume of his collected writings.

It is very interesting reading. No truly candid person meeting with it for the first time, and not previously prejudiced against it, could but be struck with its felicities of diction and its air of uncontrolled sincerity. A young man of generous impulses could scarcely, I think, read it and not fall under the spell of its sympathetic illusions. It contains unusually many of those happy phrases which are, I contend, the sole purely literary possession of Whitman. It contains dozens of those closely-packed lines in each of which Whitman contrives to concentrate a whole picture of some action or condition of Nature. It contains, perhaps, the finest, certainly the most captivating, of all Whitman's natural apostrophes :

Press close, bare-bosom'd night. Press close, magnetic, nourishing night !
Night of south winds ! night of the large few stars !
Still, nodding night ! mad, naked summer night !
Smile, O voluptuous, cool-breath'd earth !
Earth of the slumbering and liquid trees !
Earth of departed sunset ! earth of the mountains, misty-topt !
Earth of the vitreous pour of the full moon, just tinged with blue !
Earth of shine and dark, mottling the tide of the river !
Earth of the limpid grey of clouds, brighter and clearer for my sake !
Far-swooping, elbow'd earth ! rich, apple-blossom'd earth !
Smile, for your lover comes !

All this represents the best side of the author; but "Walt Whitman" exhibits his bad sides as well—his brutality, mis-styling itself openness, his toleration of the ugly and the forbidden, his terrible laxity of thought and fatuity of judgment.

If he studies "Walt Whitman" carefully, a reader of middle life will probably come to the conclusion that the best way to classify the wholly anomalous and irregular writer who produced it is to place him by himself as a maker of poems in solution. I am inclined to admit that in Walt Whitman we have just missed receiving from the New World one of the greatest of modern poets, but that we have missed it must at the same time be acknowledged. To be a poet it is not necessary to be a consistent and original thinker, with an elaborately-balanced system of ethics. The absence of intellectual quality, the superabundance of the emotional, the objective, the pictorial, are no reasons for undervaluing Whitman's imagination. But there is one condition which distinguishes art from mere amorphous expression; that condition is the result of a process through which the vague and engaging observations of Whitman never passed. He felt acutely and accurately, his imagination was purged of external impurities, he lay spread abroad in a condition of literary solution. But there he remained, an expanse of crystallisable substances, waiting for the structural change that never came; rich above almost all his coevals in the properties of poetry, and yet, for want of a definite shape and fixity, doomed to sit for ever apart from the company of the Poets.

1893.

COUNT LYOF TOLSTOI

Count Lyof Tolstoi

It has been the misfortune of Count Tolstoi to become widely known in the West of Europe at the very moment when he was performing a complete change of dress. The legitimate enthusiasm which his works of the imagination might awaken has been confused with the perhaps equally legitimate, but certainly much more obvious and vulgar surprise at the amazing character of his new social and religious views. If the alteration had taken place sooner or later, it would have been pleasanter for us and juster to him. If he had always written in a language which we could understand, we should long ago have comprehended the nature of his literary genius, and should have been less startled by his moral transformation; if the presentation to Europe had been delayed, we should have taken his work as a whole. But in point of fact, we were constantly being assured that behind the dyed curtains of that Scythian tent there sat a mysterious chieftain, arrayed in all the splendours of the Orient. We tear the veil aside at last, and discover a gentleman *in puris naturalibus*, selecting a new set of garments. It is true that this disturbing circumstance has enormously added to the fame and success of the Russian writer, and that a hundred persons are found to discuss his nakedness to one who cares to think of what he was when he was clothed. But this is little consolation to the student of pure literature, who feels inclined to drive out the social group, and to guard Count Tolstoi's doors till he has wrapped himself once more in raiment, whether civilised or savage.

Of the moral speculations of the great Russian novelist nothing shall here be said. Most of what has passed for recent criticism has occupied itself with a vain and capricious agitation of Tolstoi's views on marriage, on education, on non-resistance to authority, to the exclusion of all other considerations. It would be absurd to deny that some of these theories irresistibly invite discussion, or that the distinguished gravity of the author is not justly fascinating to an age which has been exhausted and lacerated by the funniness of its funny men. But it is difficult not to see, also, that speculation of this kind has been pursued in one form or another by every generation, that it has never yet succeeded in solving the riddle of this painful earth, and that in contrast to its evasiveness and intangibility, the positive consideration of literature as literature has a great charm. In these few words, then, Tolstoi will not be treated as the prophet or saviour of society, but as the writer of novels. For this extremely unpopular mode of regarding him, a critic's best excuse is to recall those touching and noble words written by Tourgenieff in his last hours to his great successor:

"Dearest Lyof Nikolaievitch, it is long since I wrote to you. I have been in bed, and it is my death-bed. I cannot get well; that is no longer to be thought of. I write to you expressly to assure you how happy I have been to be your contemporary, and to present to you a last, a most urgent request. Dear friend, come back to literary work! This gift came to you whence all gifts come to us. Ah! how happy should I be if I could think that you would listen to my request. My friend, great writer of our land of Russia, grant me this request."

The author of *Anna Karenine* has granted it in some degree, but how rarely, how fitfully, with how little of the artist's fire and consecration! Let us hope that in a near future he will give us of the things of the spirit in less niggardly a fashion. Let him remember that at the present moment there is no man living from whom a sane and complete work of fiction, on a large scale, would be more universally welcomed.

I

The life of the Russian novelist has often been narrated, but presents no features of very remarkable interest. Count Lyof Nikolaievitch Tolstoi was born on August 28 (o.s.), 1828, at Yasnaya Polyana, an estate on the road to Orel, a few miles out of Tula, in the centre of Russia. This place and its surroundings were described in a very charming paper contributed by Mr. Kennen to *The Century Magazine* for June 1887. Yasnaya Polyana has been the alpha and omega of Tolstoi's life, all absences from it being of the nature of episodes. He has made it his sole residence for the last thirty years, and it is the scene of his much talked-of social experiments.

Western Europe was long under the impression that Tourgenieff and Tolstoi were isolated apparitions on a bare stage. But as familiarity with Russian fiction increases in the West, we see the same structural growths proceeding in Russia as in the other countries of the world. The novel there, in its modern form, began to exist about 1840, and Gogol, whose *Dead Souls* appeared in 1842, was its creator. The "Men of the Forties," as they are called, arose out of the shadow of Gogol, and were young men when his book made its first profound sensation. The birth dates of Gontcharoff, 1813, Tourgenieff, 1818, Pisemsky, 1820, and Dostoieffsky, 1821, explain why these four illustrious novelists were aroused and fired by the publication of *Dead Souls*. It came to them, with its realism, its deep popular sympathy, and its strange humour, as a revelation at the very moment when the brain of a young man of genius is most incandescent. But Tolstoi, younger by seven years than the youngest of these, did not arrive at intellectual maturity till after the first ardour of the new life had passed away. Russia, in its rapid awakening, was a different place in 1850 from what it had been in 1840, and to understand Tolstoi aright we must distinguish him from the men of the Forties.

In endeavouring to form an idea of the literary influences which moulded his mind, we are likely to be more perplexed than aided by the strange book called *Child-*

hood, Boyhood, Youth, which bears a striking relation to the recently published autobiography of the infancy and adolescence of Pierre Loti. In each book the portrait is so different from what, one is convinced, any other person, however observant and analytical, would have made of the child in question, that one is dubious how far the tale should be looked upon as a charming and unconscious fiction. In Tolstoi the little anecdote of the imaginary dream, the incidents of which by being repeated, grew to seem absolutely true, and moved the inventor to tears of self-pity, though given as a sign of scrupulous verity in autobiography, points to a tendency which is very natural and in a novelist very fortunate.

But a strange fact is that these semi-mythical, intensely personal and curiously minute notes of the mind of a child were not made late in life, when the memory often recurs to the remotest past, but at the starting-point of the writer's career. Before he had started he stopped to look back, and he began in literature where most old men leave off. The *Childhood, Boyhood, Youth*, was commenced as early as 1851, before Tolstoi opened his brief adventure as a soldier. This book appears to be one of its author's favourites; he was long caressing it before it first appeared, and he has entirely remoulded it once, if not twice. It is excessively ingenious, and one notes with interest that the first book which attracted the future agriculturist's attention was a treatise on the growing of cabbages. The analysis of the feelings of a nervous child has seldom been carried out in a more masterly fashion. But the book is often dull,

which the author's later work can hardly be accused
of being.

II

It was Caucasia, that *Wunderland* of Russian sentiment and romance, which first awakened the imagination of Tolstoi. The Vicomte de Vogüé, in his delightful chapter on the idealism of Russia, has shown us what a Byronic fascination was exercised by the moonlit gorges of the Caucasus on the poets of seventy years ago. It was to a province steeped in romantic melancholy, penetrated by reminiscences of Pouchkine and Lermantof, that Tolstoi, a spirit of a very different order, travelled in 1851. Suddenly captured by the genius of the place, he enlisted in the army, and became an officer of artillery in a mountain fortress over the Terek. Here he began to be an author, though he published none of his Caucasian studies till he had left the Caucasus, on the breaking out of the Turkish war, in 1853. The contrast between the Asiatic and himself is the first problem which moves him in the world of fiction. Now it is illustrated by Olenine, the victim of ennui, who flings himself into the friendship of the savage Orientals; now by Jiline, who, unwillingly, and after a gallant struggle, is captured and made to live among them, but ultimately casts his chains aside; now by the gross and comfort-loving Kosteline, who pines away in the Tartar camp, and dies. In each case, though not always so romantically as in *The Cossacks*, what interests the novelist is the difference of race and instinct, rendering the inner meaning of those outward trappings whose barbaric picturesqueness tempts him to loiter on its details. Tolstoi left the Caucasus a skilful writer, expert in the conduct of a narrative, but still tinged with the blue mist of romanticism.

But he had hardly started on the three years' laborious campaign in which he was to learn so much of life, than there was published at home a book which revealed to Russian readers a new genius. *Polikouchka* was issued in 1854, the year after *The Cossacks* appeared, and if it achieved a less popular success, it deserved closer attention. It may be that Tolstoi, who has filled wider canvasses, has never painted a genre-picture more thoroughly characteristic of himself than this study of manners on a large Russian estate. *Polikouchka* is the story of a serf, who practises as a veterinary surgeon, but who is really a quack and a thief, through weakness and drink, since he is not essentially a bad fellow. His mistress, the Barina, a sentimentalist, pities him, and believes that if he went through an ordeal, on his honour, it might be the saving of him. Accordingly she sends him to a neighbouring town to fetch a large sum of money. Every one, even the man's own wife, believes that he will either steal it or squander it on drink. However, he starts, gets the money, returns faithfully, and just before reaching home loses it. Unable to face the shame of this discovery, he hangs himself, and the money is found, all safe, directly afterwards.

We may take *Polikouchka* as typical of Tolstoi's work at this time. We first notice that, although the book is short and episodical, the author has lavished upon us an astounding number of types, all sharply defined. The recruiting scene in the Mir directly points to the skill with which the vast spaces of *War and Peace* were presently to be made to swarm with human life. Then the power of sustained analysis of the complex phenomena of character, in its stranger forms, is already seen to be completely developed. The mixture of vanity, cupidity, honour and stupidity which riots in the brain of Polikouchka as he drives off to fetch the money is described with a masterly effect, and in a manner peculiar to Tolstoi. Nor is this story less typical of its author in its general construction than in its specific features. In later years, indeed, Tolstoi rarely opens a tale with the sprightly gaiety of *Polikouchka*, yet he has preserved the habit—he preserves it even in the *Kreutzer Sonata*—of beginning his stories with a scene of an amusing nature. In *Polikouchka* the tragical, the mystical element is delayed longer than has since been the author's wont, but it comes. The ghost of the suicide fingering about for the money in Doutlov's house on the fatal night is a signal for the conventionality of the tale, as a piece of literature, to break up, and this book, which began so gaily and with its feet so firmly planted on common life, closes in a scene of wild and scarcely intelligible saturnalia.

Unless I am mistaken, and no exact bibliography of

Tolstoi's writings seems to be at hand—the story which we call *Katia* (and the Russians *Conjugal Happiness*) was written while the novelist was still fighting the Turks. The extraordinary volume named *Sketches from Sevastopol* certainly belongs to this period. Totally distinct as these are—the one being a study of peaceful upper-class life on a Russian estate, the other reflecting the agitation and bewilderment of active war—they show an advance in intellectual power which takes much the same direction in either case. Tolstoi is now seen to be a clairvoyant of unexampled adroitness. If "adroit" be thought an adjective incompatible with clairvoyance, it has at least not been used here without due consideration. The peculiar quality of Tolstoi's imagination seems to require this combined attribution of the intentional and the accidental. His most amazing feats in analysis are henceforth not strictly experimental, but conjectural. The feelings of Mikhaïlov when the bomb burst, and he was wounded, may have been experienced; those of Praskouchine, who was killed, can but have been created. Few readers have not been forced to acknowledge the amazing power of the passage last alluded to. But to call it realism, in the ordinary sense, is to rob it of half its value as a singularly lofty exercise of the imagination. Yet it is precisely in this aptitude for conjectural analysis that the occasion is presented for ambition to o'ervault itself. It is the mind that sees the non-experienced quite as clearly as the experienced, which is most liable to lose consciousness of the difference between reality and unreality. The spirit that "walks upon the winds with lightness" may step into the cloud of mysticism without having noticed its presence.

III

The year 1858 was a great period of awakening in Russian fiction. It saw the publication of Gontcharoff's masterpiece, *Oblomof;* Pisemsky then rose to a height he was never to touch again in his great realistic novel, *A Thousand Souls;* Tourgenieff produced his exquisite *Assja*, and prepared the distinguished and pathetic surprise of his *Nest of Nobles*. Dostoieffsky, still away in Siberia, was putting together his notes for the *The House of the Dead*. Tolstoi, plunged for the moment in the fashionable life of St. Petersburg and Moscow, could not be ignorant of this sudden revival of letters, nor unmoved by it. Hitherto he had been content to obtain striking effects within restricted limits. If his short stories had not always closed with artistic regularity, it was that he felt the true observer's disinclination to draw the strings together artificially. But he could be contented with small spaces no longer. His mind was now set on the production of works whose proportions should be properly related to the vast and complex mass of figures which was ever moving in procession under his eyelids.

His next important publication, *Three Deaths*, which came out in 1859, resembles a bundle of studies by a great artist who contemplates a gigantic composition.

The opening description of the sick lady in her carriage, travelling in an atmosphere of eau-de-Cologne and dust, with its undemonstrative inventory of telling details, and its extreme sincerity of observation, is exactly like a page, like any page, from the two great novels which were to succeed it. But the volume is not without faults; of three selected deaths, two should scarcely have been taken from the same class of the same sex. The final picture of the conscience-smitten coachman chopping a cross is not without a certain vagueness. We hurry on, since a book awaits us which drowns *Three Deaths* as a star is drowned in the sunrise.

Tolstoi was thirty-two when he published his first great novel, *War and Peace*, in 1860. Very soon after its appearance, he took himself out of society, and began his retirement at Yasnaya Polyana. For fifteen years the world heard comparatively little of him, and then he crowned the edifice of his reputation with the successive volumes of *Anna Karenine* (1875-77). It is by these two epics of prose fiction, these massive productions, that he is mainly known. By degrees the fame of these amazing books passed beyond the ring of the Russian language, and now most educated persons in the West of Europe have read them. They dwarf all other novels by comparison. The immense area of place and time which they occupy is unexampled, and the first thing which strikes us on laying them down is their comprehensive character.

The work of no other novelist is so populous as that of Tolstoi. His books seem to include the entire existence of generations. In *War and Peace* we live with the characters through nearly a quarter of a century. They are young when we are introduced to them; we accompany them through a hundred vicissitudes of disease and health, ill fortune and good, to death or to old age. There is no other novelist, whose name I can recall, who gives anything like this sense of presenting all that moves beneath the cope of heaven. Even Stendhal is dwarfed by Tolstoi, on his own ground; and the Russian novelist joins to this anthill of the soldier and the courtier, those other worlds of Richardson, of Balzac, of Thackeray. Through each of Tolstoi's two macrocosms, thronged with highly vitalised personages, walks one man more tenderly described and vividly presented than any of the others, the figure in whom the passions of the author himself are enshrined, Pierre Bezouchof in the one case, Levine in the other. This sort of hero, to whose glorification, however, the author makes no heroic concessions, serves to give a certain solidity and continuity to the massive narration.

These two books are so widely known, that in so slight a sketch as this, their constitution may be taken as appreciated. Their magnificent fulness of life in movement, their sumptuous passages of description, their poignancy in pathos and rapidity in action, their unwavering devotion to veracity of impression, without squalor or emphasis—these qualities have given intellectual enjoyment of the highest kind to thousands of English readers. They are panoramas rather than pictures, yet finished so finely and balanced so harmoniously that we forget the immense scale upon which they are presented, in our unflagging delight in the variety and vivacity of the scene. No novelist is less the slave of a peculiarity in one of his characters than Tolstoi. He loves to take an undeveloped being, such as André in *War and Peace*, or Kitty Cherbatzky in *Anna Karenine*, and to blow upon it with all the winds of heaven, patiently noting its revulsions and advances, its inconsistencies and transitions, until the whole metamorphosis of its moral nature is complete. There is no greater proof of the extraordinary genius of Count Tolstoi than this, that through the vast evolution of his plots, his characters, though ever developing and changing, always retain their distinct individuality. The hard metal of reflected life runs ductile through the hands of this giant of the imagination.

IV

In 1877 *Anna Karenine* was finished, and the applause with which it was greeted rang from one end of Russia to the other. But the author remained in unbroken seclusion at Yasnaya Polyana. He began to write another romance on the same colossal scale, this time taking up the history of Central Europe at a point somewhat subsequent to the close of *War and Peace*. Before he had written many chapters, that crisis, that social and religious conversion ensued, which has tinctured his life and work ever since. He threw his novel aside, and, at first, he was swallowed up in didactic activity, composing those volumes on religion, education, and sociology which have created so great a stir. But he has to some slight degree, perhaps in answer to Tourgenieff's dying prayer, returned to the exercise of his talent, and has added new stories, most of them short, and most of them eccentric or mythical, to his repertory. He has composed very simple tales for children and peasants, and some of these are of a thrilling naïveté. He has written, for older readers, *A Poor Devil* and *The Death of Ivan Iliitch*.

To readers who desire a direct introduction to the work of Count Tolstoi no better volume can be recommended than that latest mentioned. It is an unsurpassed example of his naturalism, with its instinctive and yet imaginative interpretation of the most secret sentiments of the soul. It is piteously human; nay, the outcome of it all, pushed to its logical conclusion, is of a kind to break the very heart. Yet it is scarcely morbid, because wholesomely observed; nor cynical, because interpenetrated with pity and love. Ivan Iliitch is a successful lawyer, rising to a brilliant and commanding position in the world, who sickens of an obscure internal complaint, and slowly dies. His instincts, his thoughts, are followed and evenly chronicled with extreme minuteness, till all is obscured in the final misery of dissolution. The feelings of the unhappy wretch himself, of his wife, children, servants, and friends, are rendered by Tolstoi with that curious clairvoyance which we have seen to be his cardinal gift.

In reflecting upon such a book as *The Death of Ivan Iliitch*, it is natural to ask ourselves in what the realism of Tolstoi consists, and how it differs from that of M. Zola and Mr. Howells. In the first place, their habit of producing an impression by exhaustingly recording all the details which it is possible to observe is not his. Tolstoi, if they are called realists, should be styled an impressionist, not in the sense used by the artists of the present moment, but as Bastien Lepage was an impressionist in painting. If Zola and Howells fill the canvas with details to its remotest corner, Tolstoi concentrates his attention upon one figure or group, and renders the effect of that single object with a force and minute exactitude, which is positively amazing, and which far surpasses theirs. Of course, a book on such a scale as *War and Peace* would not have been conducted to a close at all if the Zola method had been brought to bear upon it. But an examination of Tolstoi's short tales will show that even when he has no need of husbanding space he adopts the same impressionist manner. With him, though observation is vivid, imagination is more vigorous still, and he cannot be tied down to describe more than he chooses to create.

This may serve to explain why his style sometimes seems so negligent, and even confused, and why his stories invariably present *lacunæ*, blank omissions where the writer has simply overlooked a series of events. The progress of Anna's mind, for example, from after her first meeting with Wronsky to the original formation of her infatuated feeling for him, is a hiatus. For some reason or other, it did not interest the novelist, and he blandly omitted to touch it. His lapses of memory, his negligence, may likewise account for the tedious and interminable length at which certain episodes are treated. There are some country scenes in *Anna Karenine*, in the course of which the author seems to have gone to sleep, and to be writing on automatically. Occasionally, Tolstoi's love of what is real leads him to distinct puerility, as in *The Story of a Horse*, where the satire, and something in the very tone of the narrator's voice remind us, but not favourably, of Hans Andersen. Yet these are slight points, and they simply indicate the limits of a very noble genius.

The realists in Russia, as well as elsewhere, have given us many good gifts—they have awakened our observation, have exposed our hallucinations, have shattered our absurd illusions. It is mere injustice to deny that they have been seekers after truth and life, and that sometimes they have touched both the one and the other. But one great gift has commonly eluded their grasp. In their struggle for reality and vividness, they have too often been brutal, or trivial, or sordid. Tolstoi is none of these. As vital as any one of them all, he is what they are not—distinguished. His radical optimism, his belief in the beauty and nobility of the human race, preserve him from the Scylla and the Charybdis of naturalism, from squalor and insipidity. They secure for his best work that quality of personal distinction which does more than anything else to give durability to imaginative literature.

1890.

CHRISTINA ROSSETTI

Christina Rossetti

WOMAN, for some reason which seems to have escaped the philosopher, has never taken a very prominent position in the history of poetry. But she has rarely been absent altogether from any great revival of poetic literature. The example of her total absence which immediately flies to the recollection is the most curious of all. That Shakespeare should have had no female rival, that the age in which music burdened every bough, and in which poets made their appearance in hundreds, should have produced not a solitary authentic poetess, even of the fifth rank, this is curious indeed. But it is as rare as curious, for though women have not often taken a very high position on Parnassus, they have seldom thus wholly absented themselves. Even in the iron age of Rome, where the Muse seemed to bring forth none but male children, we find, bound up with the savage verses of Juvenal and Persius, those seventy lines of pure and noble indignation against the brutality of Domitian which alone survive to testify to the genius of Sulpicia.

If that distinguished lady had come down to us in seventy thousand verses instead of seventy lines, would her fame have been greatly augmented? Probably not. So far as we can observe, the strength of the great poet-women has been in their selection. Not a single poetess whose fame is old enough to base a theory upon has survived in copious and versatile numbers. Men like Dryden and Victor Hugo can strike every chord of the lyre, essay every mode and species of the art, and impress us by their bulk and volume. One very gifted and ambitious Englishwoman of the last generation, Elizabeth Barrett Browning, essayed to do the same. But her success, it must be admitted, grows every day more dubious. Where she strove to be passionate she was too often hysterical; a sort of scream spoils the effect of all her full tirades. She remains readable mainly where she is exquisite, and one small volume would suffice to contain her probable bequest to posterity.

It is no new theory that women, in order to succeed in poetry, must be brief, personal, and concentrated. This was recognised by the Greek critics themselves. Into that delicious garland of the poets which was woven by Meleager to be hung outside the gate of the Gardens of the Hesperides he admits but two women from all the centuries of Hellenic song. Sappho is there, indeed, because "though her flowers were few, they were all roses," and, almost unseen, a single virginal shoot of the crocus bears the name of Erinna. That was all that womanhood gave of durable poetry to the literature of antiquity. A critic, writing five hundred years after her death, speaks of still hearing the swan-note of Erinna clear above the jangling chatter of the jays, and of still thinking those three hundred hexameter verses sung by a girl of nineteen as lovely as the loveliest of Homer's. Even at the time of the birth of Christ, Erinna's writings consisted of what could be printed on half a dozen pages of this volume. The whole of her extant work, and of Sappho's too, could now be pressed into a newspaper column. But their fame lives on, and of Sappho, at least, enough survives to prove beyond a shadow of doubt the lofty inspiration of her genius. She is the type of the woman-poet who exists not by reason of the variety or volume of her work, but by virtue of its intensity, its individuality, its artistic perfection.

At no time was it more necessary to insist on this truth than it is to-day. The multiplication of books of verse, the hackneyed character of all obvious notation of life and feeling, should, one would fancy, tend to make our poets more exiguous, more concise, and more trimly girt. There are few men nowadays from whom an immense flood of writing can be endured without fatigue; few who can hold the trumpet to their lips for hours in the market-place without making a desert around them. Yet there never was a time when the pouring out of verse was less restrained within bounds. Everything that occurs to the poet seems, to-day, to be worth writing down and printing. The result is the neglect of really good and charming work, which misses all effect because it is drowned in stuff that is second- or third-rate. The women who write, in particular, pursued by that commercial fervour which is so curious a feature of our new literary life, and which sits so inelegantly on a female figure, are in a ceaseless hurry to work off and hurry away into oblivion those qualities of their style which might, if seriously and coyly guarded, attract a permanent attention.

Among the women who have written verse in the Victorian age there is not one by whom this reproach is less deserved than it is by Miss Rossetti. Severely true to herself, an artist of conscientiousness as high as her skill is exquisite, she has never swept her fame to sea in a flood of her own outpourings. In the following pages I desire to pay no more than a just tribute of respect to one of the most perfect poets of the age— not one of the most powerful, of course, nor one of the most epoch-making, but to one of the most perfect— to a writer toward whom we may not unreasonably expect that students of English literature in the twenty-fourth century may look back as the critics of Alexandria did toward Sappho and toward Erinna.

So much has been written, since the untimely death of Dante Gabriel Rossetti, on the circumstances of his family history, that it is not requisite to enter very fully into that subject in the present sketch of his youngest sister. It is well known that the Italian poet Gabriele Rossetti, after a series of romantic adventures endured in the cause of liberty, settled in London, and married the daughter of another Italian exile, G. Polidori, Lord Byron's physician. From this stock, three-fourths of which was purely Italian, there sprang four children, of whom Dante Gabriel was the second, and Christina Georgina, born in December, 1830, the youngest. There was nothing in the training of these children which foreshadowed their various distinction in the future; although the transplanted blood ran quicker, no doubt, in veins that must now be called English, not Italian, even as the wine-red anemone broke into flower from the earth that was carried to the Campo Santo out of Palestine.

We cannot fathom these mysteries of transplantation. No doubt a thousand Italian families might settle in London, and their children be born as deaf to melody and as blind to Nature as their playfellows long native to Hoxton or Clerkenwell. Yet it is not possible to hold it quite an accident that this thousand and first family discovered in London soil the precise chemical qualities that made its Italian fibre break into clusters of blossom. Gabriel Rossetti, both as poet and painter, remained very Italian to the last, but his sister is a thorough Englishwoman. Unless I make a great mistake, she has scarcely visited Italy, and in her poetry the landscape and the observation of Nature are not only English, they are so thoroughly local that I doubt whether there is one touch in them all which proves her to have strayed more than fifty miles from London in any direction. I have no reason for saying so beyond internal evidence, but I should be inclined to suggest that the county of Sussex alone is capable of having supplied all the imagery which Miss Rossetti's poems contain. Her literary repertory, too, seems purely English; there is hardly a solitary touch in her work which betrays her transalpine parentage.

In a letter to myself, in words which she kindly lets me give to the public, Miss Rossetti has thus summed up some valuable impressions of her earliest bias toward writing:

"For me, as well as for Gabriel, whilst our 'school' was everything, it was no one definite thing. I, as the least and last of the group, may remind you that besides the clever and cultivated parents who headed us all, I in particular beheld far ahead of myself the clever sister and two clever brothers who were a little (though but a little) my seniors. And as to acquirements, I lagged out of all proportion behind them, and have never overtaken them to this day."

I interrupt my distinguished friend to remark that, even if we do not take this modest declaration with a grain of salt, it is interesting to find one more example of the fact that the possession of genius by no means presupposes a nature apt for what are called acquirements. Miss Rossetti proceeds:

"If any one thing schooled me in the direction of poetry, it was perhaps the delightful idle liberty to prowl all alone about my grandfather's cottage-grounds some thirty miles from London, entailing in my childhood a long stage-coach journey! This privilege came to an end when I was eight years old, if not earlier. The grounds were quite small, and on the simplest scale—but in those days to me they were vast, varied, worth exploring. After those charming holidays ended

I remained pent up in London till I was a great girl of fourteen, when delight reawakened at the sight of primroses in a railway cutting,—a prelude to many lovely country sights."

My impression is that a great deal of judicious neglect was practised in the Rossetti family, and that, like so many people of genius, the two poets, brother and sister, contrived to evade the educational mill. From the lips of Miss Christina herself I have it that all through her early girlhood she lay as a passive weight on the hands of those who invited her to explore those bosky groves called arithmetic, grammar, and the use of the globes. In Mr. R. L. Stevenson's little masterpiece of casuistry called *On Idlers and Idling*, he has discussed the temper of mind so sympathetically that I will say no more than this, that Philistia never will comprehend the certain fact that, to genius, Chapter VI., which is primroses in a railway cutting, is often far more important than Chapter XIII., which happens to be the subjunctive mood. But for these mysteries of education I must refer the ingenuous reader to Mr. Stevenson's delightful pages.

From her early childhood Miss Rossetti seems to have prepared herself for the occupation of her life, the art of poetry. When she was eleven her verses began to be noticed and preserved, and an extremely rare little volume, the very cynosure of Victorian bibliography, permits us to observe the development of her talent. One of the rarest of books—when it occasionally turns up at sales it commands an extravagant price—is *Verses by Christina G. Rossetti*, privately printed in 1847, at the press of her grandfather Mr. G. Polidori, "at No. 15, Park Village East, Regent's Park, London." This little volume of sixty-six pages, dedicated to the author's mother, and preceded by a pretty little preface signed by Mr. Polidori, is a curious revelation of the evolution of the poet's genius. There is hardly one piece in it which Miss Rossetti would choose to reprint in a collected edition of her works, but there are many which possess the greatest interest to a student of her mature style. The earliest verses—since all are dated—show us merely the child's desire for expression in verse, for experiment in rhyme and meter. Gradually we see the buddings of an individual manner, and in the latest piece, "The Dead City," the completion of which seems to have led to the printing of the little collection, we find the poet assuming something of her adult manner. Here are some stanzas from this rarest of booklets, which will be new, in every probability, to all my readers, and in these we detect, unmistakably, the accents of the future author of *Goblin Market*:

> *In green emerald baskets were*
> *Sun-red apples, streaked and fair;*
> *Here the nectarine and peach,*
> *And ripe plum lay, and on each*
> *The bloom rested everywhere.*
>
> *Grapes were hanging overhead,*
> *Purple, pale, and ruby-red,*

And in the panniers all around
Yellow melons shone, fresh-found,
With the dew upon them spread.

And the apricot and pear,
And the pulpy fig were there,
Cherries and dark mulberries,
Bunchy currants, strawberries,
And the lemon wan and fair.

By far the best and most characteristic of all her girlish verses, however, are those contained in a long piece entitled "Divine and Human Pleading," dated 1846. It is a pleasure to be the first to publish a passage which the author needs not blush to own after nearly fifty years, every stanza of which bears the stamp of her peculiar manner:

A woman stood beside his bed:
Her breath was fragrance all;
Round her the light was very bright,
The air was musical.

Her footsteps shone upon the stars,
Her robe was spotless white;
Her breast was radiant with the Cross,
Her head with living light.

Her eyes beamed with a sacred fire,
And on her shoulders fair,
From underneath her golden crown,
Clustered her golden hair.

Yet on her bosom her white hands
   Were folded quietly :
Yet was her glorious head bowed low
   In deep humility.

In these extracts from the volume of 1847 we see more than the germ; we see the imperfect development of two qualities which have particularly characterised the poetry of Miss Rossetti—in the first an entirely direct and vivid mode of presenting to us the impression of richly coloured physical objects, a feat in which she sometimes rivals Keats and Tennyson; and in the second a brilliant simplicity in the conduct of episodes of a visionary character, and a choice of expression which is exactly in keeping with these, a sort of Tuscan candour, as of a sacred picture in which each saint or angel is robed in a dress of one unbroken colour. These two qualities combined, in spite of their apparent incompatibility—an austere sweetness coupled with a luscious and sensuous brightness—to form one side of Miss Rossetti's curious poetic originality.

Three years later, in 1850, she was already a finished poet. That charming and pathetic failure, *The Germ*, a forlorn little periodical which attempted to emanate from the new group of Preraphaelites, as they called themselves, counted her among its original contributors. Her brother Gabriel, indeed, who had already written, in its earliest form, his remarkable poem of *The Blessed Damozel*, was the central force and prime artificer of the movement, which had begun about a

Christina Rossetti

year before. It was a moment of transition in English poetry. The old race was dying in its last representative, Wordsworth. Mr. Tennyson, Mr. Browning, Miss Barrett were the main figures of the day, while the conscience of young men and women addicted to verse was troubled with a variety of heresies, the malignity of which is hardly to be realised by us after fifty years. Mr. Bailey's *Festus* was a real power for evil, strong enough to be a momentary snare to the feet of Tennyson in writing *Maud*, and even of Browning. A host of "Spasmodists," as they were presently called, succeeded in appalling the taste of the age with their vast and shapeless tragedies, or monodramas.

Then, with a different voice, but equally far removed from the paths of correct tradition in verse, came Clough, singing in slovenly hexameters of Oxford and the pleasures of radical undergraduates in highland bothies. Clough, with his hold on reality, and his sympathetic modern accent, troubled the Preraphaelites a little; they were less moved by a far more pure and exquisite music, a song as of Simonides himself, which also reached them from Oxford, when Matthew Arnold, in 1849, made his first appearance with his lovely and long neglected *Strayed Reveller*. Mr. Coventry Patmore, with his *Poems* of 1844, was a recognised elder brother of their own, and almost everything else which was to be well done in verse for many years was to arise from among themselves, or in emulation of them. So that never was periodical better named than *The Germ*, the seed which put forth two cotyledons, and then called itself

Art and Letters; and put forth two more little leaves, and then seemed to die.

Among the anonymous contributions to the first number of *The Germ*—that for January, 1850—are two which we know to be Miss Rossetti's. These are, "Where Sunless Rivers Weep," and "Love, Strong as Death, is Dead." In the February number, under the pseudonym of Ellen Alleyn, she printed "A Pause of Thought," the song, "Oh, Roses for the Flush of Youth," and "I said of Laughter, It is Vain." To the March number, then styled *Art and Letters*, Ellen Alleyn contributed a long piece called "Repining," which does not seem to have been reprinted, and "Sweet Death" ("The Sweetest Blossoms Die"). To the fourth and last number, in which an alien and far more commonplace influence may be traced than in the others, she contributed nothing. Of her seven pieces, however, printed in *The Germ* in 1850, when she was twenty, there are five (if we omit "A Pause of Thought" and "Repining") which rank to this day among her very finest lyrics, and display her style as absolutely formed. Though the youngest poet of the confraternity, she appears indeed in *The Germ* as the most finished, and even, for the moment, the most promising, since her brother Gabriel, if the author of *The Blessed Damozel*, was also responsible for those uncouth Flemish studies in verse which he very wisely refused in later years to own or to republish.

Time passed, and the obscure group of boys and girls who called themselves Preraphaelites found themselves a centre of influence and curiosity. In poetry, as in painting and sculpture, they conquered, and more readily, perhaps, in their pupils than in themselves. The first independent publications of the school, at least, came from visitors who had been children in 1850. These books were scarcely noticed by the public; if Mr. Morris's *Defence of Guinevere* attracted a few readers in 1858, Mr. Swinburne's *Queen Mother* fell still-born from the press in 1860. These prepared the way for real and instantaneous successes—for Miss Rossetti's *Goblin Market* in 1862, for Mr. Woolner's *My Beautiful Lady* in 1863, for Mr. Swinburne's dazzling *Atalanta in Calydon* in 1865. At last, in 1870, there tardily appeared, after such expectation and tiptoe curiosity as have preceded no other book in our generation, the *Poems* of Gabriel Rossetti.

It is with these poets that Miss Rossetti takes her historical position, and their vigour and ambition had a various influence upon her style. On this side there can be no doubt that association with men so learned and eager, so daring in experiment, so well equipped in scholarship, gave her an instant and positive advantage. By nature she would seem to be of a cloistered and sequestered temper, and her genius was lifted on this wave of friendship to heights which it would not have dreamed of attempting alone. On the other hand, it is possible that, after the first moment, this association with the strongest male talent of the time has not been favourable to public appreciation of her work. Critics have taken for granted that she was a satellite, and have been puzzled to notice her divergences from the type. Of these divergences the most striking is the religious one. Neither Gabriel Rossetti, nor Mr. Swinburne, nor Mr. Morris has shown any sympathy with, or any decided interest in, the tenets of Protestantism. Now Miss Christina Rossetti's poetry is not merely Christian and Protestant, it is Anglican; nor her divine works only, but her secular also, bear the stamp of uniformity with the doctrines of the Church of England.

What is very interesting in her poetry is the union of this fixed religious faith with a hold upon physical beauty and the richer parts of Nature which allies her with her brother and with their younger friends. She does not shrink from strong delineation of the pleasures of life even when she is denouncing them. In one of the most austere of her sacred pieces, she describes the Children of the World in these glowing verses:

> *Milk-white, wine-flushed, among the vines,*
> *Up and down leaping, to and fro,*
> *Most glad, most full, made strong with wines,*
> *Blooming as peaches pearled with dew,*
> *Their golden windy hair afloat,*
> *Love-music warbling in their throat,*
> *Young men and women come and go.*

There is no literary hypocrisy here, no pretence that the apple of life is full of ashes; and this gives a startling beauty, the beauty of artistic contrast, to the poet's studies in morality. Miss Rossetti, indeed, is so didactic in the undercurrent of her mind, so anxious to adorn her tale with a religious moral, that she needs all her art, all her vigorous estimate of physical loveliness, to make her poetry delightful as poetry. That she does make it eminently delightful merely proves her extraordinary native gift. The two long pieces she has written, her two efforts at a long breath, are sustained so well as to make us regret that she has not put out her powers in the creation of a still more complete and elaborated composition. Of these two poems *Goblin Market* is by far the more popular; the other, *The Prince's Progress*, which appeared in 1866, has never attracted such attention as it deserves.

It is not necessary to describe a poem so well known to every lover of verse as *Goblin Market*. It is one of the very few purely fantastic poems of recent times which have really kept up the old tradition of humoresque literature. Its witty and fantastic conception is embroidered with fancies, descriptions, peals of laughing music, which clothe it as a queer Japanese figure may be clothed with brocade, so that the entire effect at last is beautiful and harmonious without ever having ceased to be grotesque. I confess that while I dimly perceive the underlying theme to be a didactic one, and nothing less than the sacrifice of self by a sister to recuperate a sister's virtue, I cannot follow the parable through all its delicious episodes. Like a Japanese work of art, again, one perceives the general intention, and one is satisfied with the beauty of all the detail, without comprehending or wishing to comprehend every part of the execution. For instance, the wonderful scene in which Lizzie sits beleaguered by the goblins, and receives with hard-shut mouth all the syrups that they squeeze against her skin—this from the point of view of poetry is perfect, and needs no apology or commentary; but its place in the parable it would, surely, be extremely hard to find. It is therefore, astonishing to me that the general public, that strange and unaccountable entity, has chosen to prefer *Goblin Market*, which we might conceive to be written for poets alone, to *The Prince's Progress*, where the parable and the teaching are as clear as noonday. The prince is a handsome, lazy fellow, who sets out late upon his pilgrimage, loiters in bad company by the way, is decoyed by light loves, and the hope of life, and the desire of wealth, and reaches his destined bride at last, only to find her dead. This has an obvious moral, but it is adorned with verse of the very highest romantic beauty. Every claim which criticism has to make for the singular merit of Miss Rossetti might be substantiated from this little-known romance, from which I must resist the pleasure of quoting more than a couple of stanzas descriptive of daybreak:

> *At the death of night and the birth of day,*
> *When the owl left off his sober play,*
> *And the bat hung himself out of the way,—*
>   *Woke the song of mavis and merle,*
> *And heaven put off its hodden grey*
>   *For mother-o'-pearl.*
>
> *Peeped up daisies here and there,*
> *Here, there, and everywhere;*

> *Rose a hopeful lark in the air,*
>   *Spreading out towards the sun his breast;*
> *While the moon set solemn and fair*
>   *Away in the West.*

With the apparent exceptions of *Goblin Market* and *The Prince's Progress*, both of which indeed are of a lyrical nature, Miss Rossetti has written only lyrics. All poets are unequal, except the bad ones, who are uniformly bad. Miss Rossetti indulges in the privilege which Wordsworth, Burns, and so many great masters have enjoyed, of writing extremely flat and dull poems at certain moments, and of not perceiving that they are dull or flat. She does not err in being mediocre; her lyrics are bad or good, and the ensuing remarks deal with that portion only of her poems with which criticism is occupied in surveying work so admirably original as hers, namely, that which is worthy of her reputation. Her lyrics, then, are eminent for their glow of colouring, their vivid and novel diction, and for a certain penetrating accent, whether in joy or pain, which rivets the attention. Her habitual tone is one of melancholy reverie, the pathos of which is strangely intensified by her appreciation of beauty and pleasure. There is not a chord of the minor key in "A Birthday," and yet the impression which its cumulative ecstasy leaves upon the nerves is almost pathetic:

> *My heart is like a singing-bird*
>   *Whose nest is in a watered shoot;*

My heart is like an apple-tree
 Whose boughs are bent with thick-set fruit;
My heart is like a rainbow-shell
 That paddles in a halcyon sea;
My heart is gladder than all these
 Because my love is come to me.

Raise me a dais of silk and down;
 Hang it with vair and purple dyes;
Carve it in doves and pomegranates,
 And peacocks with a hundred eyes;
Work it in gold and silver grapes,
 In leaves and silver fleurs-de-lys;
Because the birthday of my life
 Is come, my love is come to me.

It is very rarely, indeed, that the poet strikes so jubilant a note as this. Her customary music is sad, often poignantly sad. Her lyrics have that *desiderium*, that obstinate longing for something lost out of life, which Shelley's have, although her Christian faith gives her regret a more resigned and sedate character than his possesses. In the extremely rare gift of song-writing Miss Rossetti has been singularly successful. Of the poets of our time she stands next to Lord Tennyson in this branch of the art, in the spontaneous and complete quality of her *lieder*, and in their propriety for the purpose of being sung. At various times this art has flourished in our race; eighty years ago, most of the poets could write songs, but it is almost a lost art in our generation. The songs of our living poets are apt to be over-polished or under-polished, so simple as to be bald, or else so elaborate as to be wholly unsuitable for singing. But such a song as this is not unworthy to be classed with the melodies of Shakespeare, of Burns, of Shelley:

> *Oh, roses for the flush of youth,*
>   *And laurel for the perfect prime;*
> *But pluck an ivy-branch for me*
>   *Grown old before my time.*
>
> *Oh, violets for the grave of youth,*
>   *And bay for those dead in their prime;*
> *Give me the withered leaves I chose*
>   *Before in the old time.*

Her music is very delicate, and it is no small praise to her that she it is who, of living verse-writers, has left the strongest mark on the metrical nature of that miraculous artificer of verse, Mr. Swinburne. In his *Poems and Ballads*, as other critics have long ago pointed out, as was shown when that volume first appeared, several of Miss Rossetti's discoveries were transferred to his more scientific and elaborate system of harmonies, and adapted to more brilliant effects. The reader of Mr. Swinburne would judge that of all his immediate contemporaries Miss Rossetti and the late Mr. FitzGerald, the translator of *Omar Khayyám*, had been those who had influenced his style the most. Miss Rossetti, however, makes no pretence to elaborate metrical effects; she is even sometimes a little naïve, a little careless, in her rough, rhymeless endings, and metrically her work was better in her youth than it has been since.

The sonnets present points of noticeable interest. They are few, but they are of singular excellence. They have this peculiarity, that many of them are objective. Now the great bulk of good sonnets is purely subjective—occupied with reverie, with regret, with moral or religious enthusiasm. Even the celebrated sonnets of Gabriel Rossetti will be found to be mainly subjective. On the question of the relative merit of the sonnets of the brother and the sister, I hold a view in which I believe that few will at present coincide; I am certain Miss Rossetti herself will not. If she honours me by reading these pages, she may possibly recollect a conversation, far more important to me of course than to her, which we held in 1870, soon after I had first the privilege of becoming known to her. I was venturing to praise her sonnets, when she said, with the sincerity of evident conviction, that they "could only be admired before Gabriel, by printing his in the *Fortnightly Review*, showed the source of their inspiration." I was sure then, and I am certain now, that she was wrong. The sonnets are not the product of, they do not even bear any relation to those of, her brother.

Well do I recollect the publication of these sonnets of Gabriel Rossetti, in 1869, when, at a moment when curiosity regarding the mysterious painter-poet was at its height, they suddenly blossomed forth in a certain number of the *Fortnightly Review*, in whose solemn pages we were wont to see nothing lighter or more literary than esoteric politics and the prose mysteries of positivism. We were dazzled by their Italian splendour of phraseology, amazed that such sonorous anapests, that such a burst of sound, should be caged within the sober limits of the sonnet, fascinated by the tenderness of the long-drawn amorous rhetoric; but there were some of us who soon recovered an equilibrium of taste, in which it seemed that the tradition of the English sonnet, its elegance of phrase, its decorum of movement, were too rudely displaced by this brilliant Italian intruder, and that underneath the melody and the glowing diction, the actual thought, the valuable and intelligible residue of poetry, was too often much more thin than Rossetti allowed it to be in the best of his other poems. As to Gabriel Rossetti's sonnets being his own best work, as has been asserted, I for one must entirely and finally disagree. I believe that of all his poetry they form the section which will be the first to tarnish. Quite otherwise is it with Miss Christina Rossetti. It is in certain of her objective sonnets that her touch is most firm and picturesque, her intelligence most weighty, and her style most completely characteristic. The reader need but turn to "After Death," "On the Wing," "Venus's Looking-Glass" (in the volume of 1875), and the marvellous "A Triad"* to concede the truth of this; while in the

---

* Why has Miss Rossetti allowed this piece, one of the gems of the volume of 1862, to drop out of her collected poems?

more obvious subjective manner of sonnet-writing she is one of the most successful poets of our time. In "The World," where she may be held to come closest to her brother as a sonneteer, she seems to me to surpass him.

From the first a large section of Miss Rossetti's work has been occupied with sacred and devotional themes. Through this most rare and difficult department of the art, which so few essay without breaking on the Scylla of doctrine on the one hand, or being whirled in the Charybdis of commonplace dulness on the other, she has steered with extraordinary success. Her sacred poems are truly sacred, and yet not unpoetical. As a religious poet of our time she has no rival but Cardinal Newman, and it could only be schismatic prejudice or absence of critical faculty which should deny her a place, as a poet, higher than that of our exquisite master of prose. To find her exact parallel it is at once her strength and her snare that we must go back to the middle of the seventeenth century. She is the sister of George Herbert; she is of the family of Crashaw, of Vaughan, of Wither. The metrical address of Herbert has been perilously attractive to her; the broken stanzas of "Consider" or of "Long Barren" remind us of the age when pious aspirations took the form of wings, or hour-glasses, or lamps of the temple. The most thrilling and spirited of her sacred poems have been free from these Marini-like subtleties. There is only what is best in the quaint and fervent school of Herbert visible in such pieces as "The Three Enemies," "A

Rose Plant in Jericho," "Passing Away, saith the World," and " Up Hill." Still more completely satisfactory, perhaps, is " Amor Mundi," first included in the *Poems* of 1875, which takes rank as one of the most solemn, imaginative, and powerful lyrics on a purely religious subject ever printed in England.

These critical and biographical remarks were mainly written in 1882, but not printed until 1893. They were undertaken at the suggestion of Dante Gabriel Rossetti, who was kind enough to consider that I had an appreciation of his sister such as is more common now than fourteen years ago. They were scarcely finished when the news came of his death, and in the agitation produced by that event, I thought it better to put aside for a time my criticism of Christina.

It will, perhaps, be not inappropriate for me to record here my few personal recollections of this illustrious lady. It was not my privilege to meet her more than some dozen times in the flesh, and those times mainly in the winter of 1870-71. But on most of those occasions I had the good fortune to converse with her for a long while; and up to a few months before her death we corresponded at not particularly distant intervals. She is known to the world, and very happily known, by her brother's portraits of her, and in particular by the singularly beautiful chalk drawing in profile, dated 1866. I think that tasteful arrangement of dress might have made her appear a noble and even a romantic figure so late as 1870, but, as I suppose, an ascetic or almost methodistical reserve caused her to clothe herself in a style, or with an absence of style, which was really distressing; her dark hair was streaked across her olive forehead, and turned up in a chignon; the high stiff dress ended in a hard collar and plain brooch, the extraordinarily ordinary skirt sank over a belated crinoline, and these were inflictions hard to bear from the high-priestess of Preraphaelitism. When it is added that her manner, from shyness, was of a portentous solemnity, that she had no small talk whatever, and that the common topics of the day appeared to be entirely unknown to her, it will be understood that she was considered highly formidable by the young and the flighty. I have seen her sitting alone, in the midst of a noisy drawing-room, like a pillar of cloud, a Sibyl whom no one had the audacity to approach.

Yet a kinder or simpler soul, or one less concentrated on self, or of a humbler sweetness, never existed. And to an enthusiast, who broke the bar of conventional chatter, and ventured on real subjects, her heart seemed to open like an unsealed fountain. The heavy lids of her weary-looking, bistred, Italian eyes would lift and display her ardour as she talked of the mysteries of poetry and religion. My visits to her, in her mother's house, 56 Euston Square, were abruptly brought to a close. On May 1, 1871, I received a note from her elder sister Maria warning me not to dine with them on the following Tuesday, as her sister was suddenly and alarmingly ill. This was, in fact, the mysterious complaint which thenceforth kept Christina bedridden, and sometimes at the point of death, for two years. She recovered, but the next time I saw her—she was well enough to be working in the British Museum in the summer of 1873—she was so strangely altered as to be scarcely recognisable.

By degrees, to my great satisfaction, Miss Christina came to look upon me as in some little sense her champion in the press. "The pen you use for me has always a soft rather than a hard nib," she said, and in truth, whenever I found an opportunity of praising her pure and admirable poems, I was not slow to employ it. That I was not exempt, however, from an occasional peck even from this gentlest of turtle-doves, a letter (written in December 1875) reminds me. I had reviewed somewhere the first collected edition of her *Poems*, and I had ventured to make certain reservations. There are some points of valuable self-analysis which make a part of this letter proper to be quoted here :

"Save me from my friends! You are certainly up in your subject, and as I *might* have fared worse in other hands I will not regret that rival reviewer [Mr. Theodore Watts] who was hindered from saying his say. As to the lamented early lyrics, I do not suppose myself to be the person least tenderly reminiscent of them [I had grumbled at the excision of some admirable favourites]; but it at any rate appears to be the commoner fault amongst verse-writers to write what is not worth writing, than to suppress what would merit hearers. I for my part am a great believer in the genuine poetic impulse belonging (very often) to the spring and not to the autumn of life, and some established reputations fail to shake me in this opinion; at any rate, if so one feels the possibility to stand in one's own case, then I vote that the grace of silence succeed the grace of song. By all which I do not bind myself to unbroken silence, but meanwhile I defend my position—or, you may retort, I do not defend it. By-the-by, your *upness* does not prevent my protesting that Edith and Maggie did not dream or even nap; *Flora* did; but have I not caught *you* napping? Do, pray, come and see me and we will not fight."

It is difficult to speak of either of the Rossetti ladies without a reference to the elder sister, whom also I had the privilege of knowing in early days. She left upon me the impression of stronger character, though of narrower intellect and infinitely poorer imagination. I formed the idea, I know not whether with justice, that the pronounced high-church views of Maria, who throve on ritual, starved the less pietistic, but painfully conscientious nature of Christina. The influence of Maria Francesca Rossetti on her sister seemed to be like that of Newton upon Cowper, a species of police surveillance exercised by a hard, convinced mind over a softer and more fanciful one. Miss Maria Rossetti, who generally needed the name of Dante to awaken her from a certain social torpor, died in 1876, but not until she had set her seal on the religious habits of her sister. Such, at least, was the notion which I formed, perhaps on slight premises.

That the conscience of the younger sister was, in middle life, so tender as to appear almost morbid, no one, I think, will deny. I recall an amusing instance of it. In the winter of 1874, I was asked to secure some influential signatures to a petition against the destruction of a part of the New Forest. Mr. Swinburne promised me his, if I could induce Miss Christina Rossetti to give hers, suggesting as he did so, that the feat might not be an easy one. In fact, I found that no little palaver was necessary; but at last she was so far persuaded of the innocence of the protest that she wrote *Chr;* she then stopped, dropped the pen, and said very earnestly, "Are you sure that they do not propose to build churches on the land?" After a long time, I succeeded in convincing her that such a scheme was not thought of, and she proceeded to write *istina G. Ros*, and stopped again. "Nor schoolhouses?" fluctuating with tremulous scruple. At length she finished the signature, and I carried the parchment off to claim the fulfilment of Mr. Swinburne's promise. And the labourer felt that he was worthy of his hire.

On the 6th of July, 1876, I saw Christina Rossetti for the last time. I suppose that her life, during the last twenty years of it, was as sequestered as that of any pious woman in a religious house. She stirred but little, I fancy, from her rooms save to attend the services of the Anglican church. That her mind continued humane and simple her successive publications and her kind and sometimes playful letters proved.

Misfortunes attended her family, and she who had been the centre of so eager and vivid a group, lived to find herself almost solitary. At length, on the 29th of December, 1894, after prolonged sufferings borne with infinite patience, this great writer, who was also a great saint, passed into the region of her visions.

LORD DE TABLEY

Lord De Tabley

A PORTRAIT

It will not be disputed, I think, by any one who enjoyed the friendship of the third Lord De Tabley that no more singular, more complicated, more pathetic nature has been—I dare not say revealed—but indicated to us in these late times. His mind was like a jewel with innumerable facets, all slightly blurred or misted; or perhaps it would be a juster illustration to compare his character to an opal, where all the colours lie perdue, drowned in a milky mystery, and so arranged that to a couple of observers, simultaneously bending over it, the prevalent hue shall in one case seem a pale green, in the other a fiery crimson. This complication of Lord De Tabley's emotional experience, the ardour of his designs, the languor of his performance, the astonishing breadth and variety of his sympathies, his intense personal reserve, the feverish activity of his intellectual life, the universality of his knowledge, like that of a magician, the abysses of his ignorance, like those of a child, all these contrary elements fused in and veiled by a sort of radiant dimness, made his nature one of the most extraordinary, because the most inscrutable, that I have ever known. Tennyson said to me of Lord De Tabley, in 1888, "He is Faunus; he is a woodland creature!" That was one aspect, noted with great acumen. But that was a single aspect. He was also a scholar of extreme elegance, a numismatist and a botanist of exact and minute accomplishment, the shyest of recluses, the most playful of companions, the most melancholy of solitaries, above all and most of all, yet in a curiously phantasmal way, a poet. It would need the hand of Balzac to draw together into a portrait threads so slight, so delicately elastic, and so intricately intertwined. When all should be said, however, in the most fastidious language, something would escape, and that would be the essential being of the strangest and the most shadowy of men.

I

John Byrne Leicester Warren, the third and last Baron De Tabley, was born at Tabley House, Cheshire, on April 26, 1835. He was the eldest son, and his mother, Catherina Barbara, daughter of Jerome, Count De Salis, from whom he inherited his sensibility and his imagination, gave, I have heard, to the ceremony of his baptism something of a romantic character, his godfather, Lord Zouche, having brought water from the river Jordan for the christening. For the first twelve or thirteen years of his life, until he went to Eton, indeed, he lived mostly with his mother in the south of Europe, and faint impressions of this childish exile seemed to be always returning to him in later life.

In these early days in Italy and Germany the foundation was laid of his love of botany, coins, minerals, and fine art, by the companionship of his godfather, then Robert Curzon, who travelled with his parents, and who bought for them the beautiful Italian things—enamels, majolica, medals, and statuettes—which are now the ornament of Tabley House. He was a finished connoisseur, and in his company the little Johnny visited old shops and museums, eager to begin, at ten years of age, a collection of his own. He was meanwhile being very carefully prepared for Eton.

In 1845 the death of his younger brother made centre about John Warren the hopes of the family, and no more male children were born to his father. From Eton he proceeded to Christ Church, Oxford. Among his close Oxford friends, there survive Sir Henry Longley, who is now his executor, and Sir Baldwyn Leighton, who, in 1864, became his brother-in-law. Henry Cowper, Lord Edward Clinton, and the late Lord Lothian were among his close companions. Prince Frederick of Holstein, who died some ten years ago, was a very great friend up to the last. But by far the dearest of his college intimates was George Fortescue, a young man of extraordinary promise, a few weeks older than himself, who awakened in Warren the passion for poetry, and was all to him that Arthur Hallam was to Tennyson. Fortescue would, perhaps, have been a poet had he lived; at all events, the two friends wrote verses in secret, and, as shall presently be told, in secret published them. This delightful association, however, was suddenly snapped; on November 2, 1859, George Fortescue lost his footing while climbing a mast on board the yacht of the late Earl of Drogheda in the Mediterranean, fell, and was killed. This incident was one from which John Warren never entirely recovered; after the first agony of grief he mentioned his friend no more, and would fain have obliterated his very memory.

Before this deplorable catastrophe, however, Warren had entered life. He had taken his degree in 1856, with a double second-class in classics and modern history. In the autumn of 1858 Lord Stratford de Redcliffe, going out to Turkey for the last time, to bid farewell to the Sultan, was permitted to take with him three unpaid temporary attachés. He chose John Warren, Lord Sandwich (then Lord Hinchinbrooke), and Mr. J. R. Swinton, the portrait-painter. The visit to Constantinople was, on the whole, fairly agreeable. Warren made the acquaintance of Lord Strangford, with whom he found himself infinitely in sympathy, and whose close friend he remained until Lord Strangford's untimely death. He went reluctantly, but Lord Strangford's companionship was a joy to him, and as numismatics were now the passion of his life, he was able to dig in the Troad for the coins of Asia Minor, and to scour the bazaars of Stamboul for Greek federal moneys. The months spent in Turkey were not without stimulus and interest; unhappily he suffered from dysentery and had to come home. This disease he never entirely conquered; only the other day he wrote from Ryde, "I am just as bad as I was with the Cannings at Constantinople."

After his return to England, the shock of Fortescue's death at first unfitted him for all mental exertion. But he struggled against his unhappiness, continued his numismatic studies, seriously determined to become a poet, and began to see a little more of that Cheshire life, in his father's noble old house, which hitherto he had known so little. His talents attracted the attention of family friends and neighbours, such as Mr. Gladstone and Lord Houghton, with both of whom, but especially with the former, he became on intimate terms. He was called to the Bar in 1860. The Cheshire Yeomanry had its headquarters in Tabley Park, and John Warren was first an officer in, and then captain of it, until he came into the title in 1887, when, to the regret of the neighbourhood, he gave up this local interest. All these things will sound strange to those who only knew Lord De Tabley as a poet; still stranger to those who knew him as a man may sound the fact that in 1868, urged by his father, and under the particular ægis of Mr. Gladstone, he unsuccessfully contested Mid-Cheshire in the Liberal interest. What is less known is that, a little while before Mr. Gladstone's first Home Rule Bill, Warren had determined to try for a seat again; but events presently converted him into a Liberal Unionist. At his father's second marriage in 1871, he left his home in Cheshire, and went to reside in London.

In the later sixties, when he was more and more devoting himself to poetry and science, he was less of of a recluse than at any other period of his life. After the publication of his *Philoctetes* in 1867, the late Lord Houghton introduced him to Tennyson, who was always a warm admirer of his poetry. Warren's acquaintance with Tennyson became almost intimate for seven or eight years, although he could not quite get over a certain terror of that formidable bard. (After 1880, I think, he never saw him.) Several incidents, among which I will only mention the death of his mother in February 1869, and of his sister, Lady Bathurst, in 1872, tended to deepen and irritate his melancholy, which had already become chronic when I first knew him in 1875. Suc cessive annoyances and disappointments so fostered this condition, that about 1880 he practically disappeared. That was the beginning of the time to which Sir Mountstuart Grant Duff refers, in the valuable and interesting notice of De Tabley which he contributed to the *Spectator* of December 7, 1895, when he says that people declared "Warren has two intimate friends. The first he has not seen for five years, the second for six."

The death of his father, in 1887, roused him from his social lethargy. He found the estate practically insolvent, and only by the sacrifice of the whole of his own private fortune, and the greatest economy during the remainder of his life, was he able to prevent the sale and secure the retention of the family mansion. In 1893 the success of his *Poems* gave him an instant of fame, which greatly comforted and cheered him. That year was probably, on the whole, the brightest of his life. But he was already looking old, and those who have seen him ever since at short intervals must have noticed how rapidly he was ageing and weakening. When, this last summer, he lunched with me to meet Mr. Bailey, the author of *Festus*, a man more than twenty years his senior, I could but wonder whether any stranger could have conceived Lord De Tabley to be the younger. All this autumn his face had the solemn Trophonian pallor, the look of the man who has seen Death in the cave. Yet the end was unexpected. He was planning to spend the winter at Bournemouth with his sister, Lady Leighton, but lingered on, as his wont was, in his lodgings at Ryde. He was positively ill but a day or two, sinking rapidly, and passing away, without suffering, on November 22, 1895, in his sixty-first year. The coffin was brought to his beautiful home in Cheshire, and buried in the grass of Little Peover churchyard, where he had wished to lie. Earth from the Holy Land was sprinkled over him, and the grave was filled up with clods from a certain covert where he had loved to botanise. Such is the meagre outline of a life, whose adventures were almost wholly those of the soul.

II

John Warren's first enterprise in the world of published poetry was a very obscure little volume, issued in 1859, under the title of *Poems. By G. F. Preston.*

A rarer volume scarcely exists, for nobody bought it, and almost every copy disappeared, or was destroyed. It is a mere curiosity, for it contains not a single piece that deserves to live, although it is interesting to find in it several subjects and titles which Warren afterwards used again. Immense is the advance, in every direction, marked by *Praeterita*, a volume entirely by Warren, published in 1863, under another pseudonym, "William Lancaster." The moment was not favourable to the issue of poetry of a contemplative and descriptive order. Mrs. Browning and Clough were lately dead; Tennyson, while preparing the *Enoch Arden* volume, had published nothing since *The Idylls of the King;* Matthew Arnold, who appeared to have given up the practice of poetry, in which no one encouraged him, was a professor at Oxford; Robert Browning had been silent since the cold reception of *Men and Women*. It was a dead time, before the revival and wild revels of the Preraphaelites. No verse that was not smoothly Tennysonian and mildly idyllic was in favour with the public.

Warren's modest volume had no success, nor is it probable that it has ever possessed more than a very few readers. Yet its merits should have been patent to at least one reviewer. The splendour of diction which was afterwards to distinguish his poetry Warren had not yet discovered. *Praeterita* is noticeable mainly for two qualities—for the close and individual observation of natural phenomena, in which not even Tennyson excelled Lord De Tabley, and for the technical beauty of the blank verse pieces, which are usually better made than the lyrical. Of the former of those qualities specimens may be given almost at random, as this of a frosty day in the country:

> *When the waves are solid floor,*
> *And the clods are iron-bound,*
> *And the boughs are crystall'd hoar,*
> *And the red leaf nailed aground;*
>
> *When the fieldfare's flight is slow,*
> *And a rosy vapour-rim,*
> *Now the sun is small and low,*
> *Belts along the region dim;*
>
> *When the ice-crack flies and flaws,*
> *Shore to shore, with thunder shock,*
> *Deeper than the evening daws,*
> *Clearer than the village clock.*

(De Tabley was, like Wordsworth, a bold and graceful skater, and used, it is said, to cut his own name in full on the ice of Tabley Lake without pausing); or this description of dawn:

> *ere heaven's stubborn bar and subtle screen*
> *Crumbled in purple chains of sailing shower*
> *And bared the captive morning in his cell;*

while his mosaic of delicate and minute observation of aërial phenomena is displayed in conjunction with the excellence of his blank verse in this study of "tremulous evening":

> *The weeds of night coast round her lucid edge,*
> *Yoked under bulks of tributary cloud;*
> *The leaves are shaken on the forest flowers,*
> *And silent as the silence of a shrine*
> *Lies a great power of sunset on the groves.*
> *Greyly the fingered shadows dwell between*
> *The reaching chestnut-branches. Grey the mask*
> *Of twilight, and the bleak unmellow speed*
> *Of blindness on the visage of fresh hills.*

Here every epithet is felt, is observed; and the volume is full of such pictures and of such verse. Nevertheless, the book is not interesting; its beauties are easily overlooked, and we feel, in glancing back, that it gave an inadequate impression of its author's powers. Similar characteristics marked the volumes called *Eclogues and Monodramas* and *Studies in Verse*.

Then came the publication of *Atalanta in Calydon*, and Warren's eyes were dazzled with the emergence of this blazing luminary from the Oxford horizon, which he had himself so lately left.

Of Mr. Swinburne's influence on Warren's imagination, on his whole intellectual character, there can be no question. Personal influence there was none; he recollected, dimly, the brilliant boy at Eton, two years his junior; and once, in 1877, I persuaded these two men, of talents and habits of mind so diverse, to meet at dinner in my house; with that exception—and Warren was absolutely tongue-tied throughout the eventful evening—he never (I think) saw the poet whose work had so deeply ploughed up his prejudices and traditions. But he had been one of the very first to read *Atalanta,* and he had tormented G. H. Lewes into a grudging permission to let him write about it in the *Fortnightly Review.* His article appeared, and was one of those which earliest called attention to Mr. Swinburne's genius; but Lewes, although Warren's criticism was signed, had toned down the ardour of it, and had introduced one or two slighting phrases. These editorial corrections poor Warren carried about with him, like open wounds, for, it is no exaggeration to say, thirty years, and to the last could never be reminded of Mr. Swinburne without a shudder at the thought of what he must think that Warren thought he thought. Alas! at times his life was made a perfect nightmare to him by reverberated sensibilities of this kind.

The importance of the stimulus given to Warren by Mr. Swinburne's early publications was seen in the metrical drama after the antique, *Philoctetes,* printed in 1867. It was announced as "by M.A.," which meant Master of Arts, a further excess of anonymity, but which was interpreted as meaning Matthew Arnold, to the author's unfeigned dismay. This rumour—instantly contradicted, of course—gave a certain piquancy to the book, and this was the one of all Warren's early volumes which may be said to have received an adequate welcome. It was compared with *Merope,* and its superiority to that frigid fiasco was patent. In *Philoctetes* Warren, undisturbed by the circumstance that Sophocles had taken the same story for one of the most stately of his tragedies, undertook to develop the character of the wounded exile in his solitary cave in Lemnos, and under the wiles of Ulysses. In the poem of Sophocles no woman is introduced, but Warren creates Ægle, a girl of the island, humbly devoted to Philoctetes. Instead of the beautiful, delicate Neoptolemus of Sophocles, the modern poet makes the companion of Ulysses a rougher figure, and omits Heracles altogether. This plot, indeed, is quite independent of that of Sophocles. He introduces a chorus of fishermen, who chant unrhymed odes, often of extreme beauty, in this manner:

> *Pan is a god seated in nature's cave,*
> *Abiding with us,*
> *No cloudy ruler in the delicate air-belts,*
> *But in the ripening slips and tangles*
> *Of cork-woods, in the bull-rush pits where oxen*
> *Lie soaking, chin-deep;*
> *In the mulberry-orchard,*
> *With milky kexes and marrowy hemlocks,*
> *Among the floating silken under-darnels.*
> *He is a god, this Pan,*
> *Content to dwell among us, nor disdains*
> *The damp, hot wood-smell;*
> *He loves the flakey pine-boles sand-brown.*

To give any impression of a tragical drama by brief extracts is impossible. But Warren put a great deal of himself into the soliloquies of the lame warrior, and few who knew him but will recognise a self-conscious portrait when Ulysses tells his companion that

Persuasion, Pyrrhus, is a delicate thing,
And very intricate the toil of words
Whereby to smoothe away the spiteful past
From a proud heart on edge with long disease;
For round the sick man, like a poison'd mist,
His wrongs are ever brooding. He cannot shake
These insects of the shadow from his brow
In the free bountiful air of enterprize.
Therefore expect reproaches of this man
And bitter spurts of anger; for much pain
Hath nothing healed his wound these many years.

The publication of *Philoctetes*, however, marks a period of healing almost like that of the Lemnian hero's own return. The shy and self-distrusting poet was conscious of a warm tide of encouragement. From many sides greetings flowed in upon him. Tennyson, though deprecating the composition of antique choral dramas as not a natural form of art, applauded; Robert Browning was enthusiastic; Mr. Gladstone, an old family friend, was warm in congratulation. This was the one bright moment in Warren's early literary life; something like fame seemed to reach him for a moment, and his delicate, shy nature expanded in the glow of it. It passed as quickly as it came, and a quarter of a century was to go by, and nearly the whole remaining period of his life, before he tasted popular praise again.

Encouraged by this ephemeral success and applause, and under the stress of a violent and complicated private emotion, Warren wrote in 1868 another antique drama, his *Orestes*, in my judgment the most completely satisfactory of his works, and the most original. It was not, however, well received. The classical reviewers were stupefied to discover that the hero was not the celebrated son of Agamemnon, but a wholly fictitious Orestes, "prince of the Larissæan branch of the Aleuadæ." This fact alienated sympathy while it puzzled the critics, who received with frigid caution a play, the plot of which seemed to lay a trap for their feet. Why Warren, with characteristic lack of literary tact, chose the unhappy name of Orestes for his hero, I know not; when it was too late, he bewailed his imprudence. But the reception of this noble poem—which, some day or other, must be re-discovered and read—was one of the tragical events in Warren's life. This should, too, have been the moment for him to drop the veil, and come forward in his real person; but all he could persuade himself to concede was a return to the old unmeaning pseudonymn, "William Lancaster."

The neglect was trebly undeserved. *Orestes* was one of the most beautiful poems that English literature produced between the generation of Arnold and that of Rossetti. The plot is simple, dignified, and dramatic, the verse strong and vivid, well-knit, and not of a too-waxy sweetness. There is a scene near the close—where Orestes, who has discovered that his mother, Dyseris, is dishonoured in the love of Simus, an adventurer, turns upon her, breaking the chain of filial awe, and denounces her crimes to her face, going too far, indeed, and accusing her, falsely, of a design upon his own life—which is magnificent, with the stately, large passion of Racine. It is unfortunate that to quote intelligibly any of this species of poetry demands a wider space than can here be spared. But I hope that whatever revival of Lord De Tabley's poetry may be made, will without fail include *Orestes*.

In the next years he essayed, still as William Lancaster, to write novels. He made no mark, though, I believe, a little money, by *A Screw Loose*, 1868, and *Ropes of Sand*, 1869. He returned to his true vocation in the volume of poems entitled *Rehearsals*, 1870, when for the first time a title-page carried the full name John Leicester Warren. *Searching the Net* followed in 1873, and we may take these two books together, for they were identical in character, and they displayed the poet at his average level of execution. In these dramatic monologues, songs, odes, and sonnets we find a talent, which in its essence was exquisite, struggling against a variety of disadvantages. Among these—and it is necessary to mention them, for they were always Lord De Tabley's persistent enemies—two were peculiarly prominent, want of concentration and want of critical taste. The importance of the first-mentioned quality, in his case, was exemplified by the success of the volume of 1893, which mainly consisted of the best things, and nothing but the best, which he had previously published. The second led him to produce and to print what was not reprinted in 1893, and to give it just as much prominence as he gave his best pieces. Nothing else will account for the neglect of such things as lie strewn about the pages of these unequal volumes, pictures like :

> *Where deep woods swoon with solitude divine,*
> *I wait thee there, arm-deep in flowery twine,*
> *Where gleam flushed poppies in among grey tares;*
> *Grape-clusters mellow near, and tumbled pears*
> *Are brown in orchard-grass. The fern-owl calls*
> *At eve across the cloven river-falls,*
> *Whose flood leaves here an island, there a swan.*

Or this, from the fine dramatic fragment called "Medea":

> *The sullen king turns roughly on his heel,*
> *Whirling his regal mantle round his eyes,*
> *And so departs, with slow steps, obstinate;*
> *Ah, but the queen, the pale one, beautiful,*
> *Prone, in the dust her holy bosom laid,*
> *Mingles her outspread hair with fallen leaves,*
> *And sandal-soil is on her gracious head.*
> *Ah, lamentable lady, pitiful!*

Warren's next work was a drama, on which he was working long, and from which he expected much. But *The Soldier of Fortune*, 1876, proved the worst of his literary disasters. It was a vague German story of the sixteenth century put into blank verse, and cut into five huge acts; this "play" extends to between four and five hundred pages. It is essentially undramatic, mere bed-rock, through which run veins of pure gold of poetry, but in an impregnable condition. *The Soldier of Fortune* is full of beautiful lines, one of which, in particular, has always run in my memory—

On worm-drill'd vellums of ld-time revenges,—

but it is perfectly hopeless as a piece of literature. He told me lately—I know not whether in pardonable exaggeration—that not a single copy of it was sold. He was deeply irritated and wounded, and now began that retirement from the public which lasted obstinately for seventeen years.

At last his brother-in-law, Sir Baldwyn Leighton, persuaded him that a new generation had arisen, to whom he might make a fresh appeal. Others encouraged this idea, and by degrees the notion that a selection of the best things in his old books, supplemented by what he had written during these years of eclipse, might form a volume which people would read with pleasure. The result was *Poems Dramatic and Lyrical*, of 1893, which still represents Lord De Tabley to the majority of readers. This book enjoyed a genuine and substantial success, quite as great as verse of this stately order could enjoy. He was encouraged to write more, and, to our general astonishment, he was able, in the spring of 1895, to produce, in identical form, a second series of the *Poems*. This was respectfully received, but so enthusiastic a welcome as greeted the concentrated selection of 1893 was hardly to be looked for.

From the new poems in the volume of 1893 a fragment of that entitled "Circe" may here be quoted:

>   *Reared across a loom,*
> *Hung a fair web of tapestry half done,*
> *Crowding with folds and fancies half the room:*
> *Men eyed as gods, and damsels still as stone*
> *Pressing their brows alone,*
> *In amethystine robes,*
> *Or reaching at the polished orchard-globes,*
> *Or rubbing parted love-lips on their rind,*
> *While the wind*
> *Sows with sere apple-leaves their breast and hair;*
> *And all the margin there*
> *Was arabesqued and bordered intricate*
> *With hairy spider-things*
> *That catch and clamber,*
> And salamander in his dripping-cave,
> Satanic ebon-amber;
> *Blind-worm, and asp, and eft of cumbrous gait,*
> *And toads who love rank grasses near a grave,*
> And the great goblin moth, who bears
> Between his wings the ruined eyes of death;
> *And the enamelled sails*
> *Of butterflies who watch the morning's breath,*
> *And many an emerald lizard with quick ears,*
> *Asleep in rocky dales;*
> *And for an outer fringe embroidered small,*
> *A ring of many locusts, horny-coated,*
> *A round of chirping tree-frogs merry-throated,*
> *And sly, fat fishes sailing, watching all.*

This sumptuous picture, a sort of Shield of Achilles in a fragment of an epic, is very strongly composed.

If we examine the central and typical qualities of

Lord De Tabley as a poet, we are struck first by the brocaded magnificence of his style. This steadily grew with his growth, and was an element of real originality. It is to be distinguished from anything like tinsel or flash in what he wrote; it was a genuine thing, fostered, in later years, by a very close study of the diction of Milton, which gave him more and more delight as he grew older. He liked to wrap his thought in cloth of gold, to select from the immense repertory of his memory the most gorgeously sonorous noun, the most imperial adjective, at his command. In all this he was consciously out of sympathy with the men of our own time, who prefer the rougher, directer verbiage, or else a studied simplicity. The poetry of Lord De Tabley was not simple; when he tried to make it homely, he utterly failed. His efforts at humour, at naïve pathos, were generally unfortunate. But, when his melancholy, dignified Muse stalked across the stage wrapped in heavy robes, stiff with threads of gold, she rose to her full stature and asserted her personal dignity with success. It was with the gorgeous writers of the middle of the seventeenth century that Lord De Tabley found himself in fullest sympathy, with Milton and Crashaw in verse, with Jeremy Taylor and Sir Thomas Browne in prose. So, among poets of the present century, his sympathies were all with Keats and Browning, while for Wordsworth and Matthew Arnold he had a positive indifference; he liked a weighty form and full colour in style, and it was in the production of such a manner that he excelled.

Another central quality which distinguishes him as a poet is his extremely minute and accurate observation of natural phenomena. Many poets of a high order recognise no flower but the rose, and no bird but the nightingale, and are fortunate if the whale is not their only fish. But among his exceptional accomplishments, Lord De Tabley counted an exact knowledge of several branches of science. In botany, in particular, and in ornithology, his reputation at certain points was European; I believe I am right, for instance, in saying that he was the first living authority on the Brambles. His eye, trained in many branches of observation, served him admirably as a poet; for the general reader, it served him, perhaps, too well, bewildering the untaught brain with the frequency and the exactitude of his images drawn from the visible world of earth and sky. In these he is not less accurate than Tennyson, and he sometimes pushes his note of nature still further into elaborate portraitures of country life than Tennyson, with greater tact, ever cared to do.

If I am asked to say, at once, wherein I consider that the strength and weakness alike of this poet consisted, I reply in his treatment of detail. His theory of execution was one in which detail took a paramount place. Jewels five words long were what he delighted in and desired to produce, and to secure them he sacrificed the general rotundity and perfection of his work. In this, as in certain other points, he resembled the great Jacobean poets. Like Cyril Tourneur, or like Giles Fletcher, to mention two very dissimilar writers, with each of whom he presented certain analogies, he was so fascinated with a single line that was specially exquisite or thrilling, a single image which was novel and picturesque, that he was content to leave it set in a ragged passage which was almost wholly without charm. He even seemed, as they often seem, to prefer to wear his rubies and opals on a dingy texture that they might beam from it more radiantly. The splendid single line is out of fashion now—fifty years ago it was absolutely dominant in English poetry—and Lord De Tabley's resolute cultivation of it gave his verse an old-fashioned air. We are just now all in favour of a poetry in which the force and beauty are equally distributed throughout, and in which execution, not of a line or of a stanza, but of a complete poem, is aimed at. But this is really a fashion rather than a law.

III

In some dedicatory verses to myself, which Lord De Tabley printed in 1893, he said that "twenty years and more" were then "ended" since the beginning of our friendship. His memory slightly stretched the period, but it was in the winter of 1875 that I met him first. I have no recollection of the event; one week I had never heard of him, the next week he had become part of my existence. Long afterwards he told me that, crossing Hyde Park one Sunday morning, after a painful interview with an old companion, he had observed to himself that his acquaintances had fallen below the number which he could count on the fingers of his two hands; his principle was that one should not be acquainted with fewer than ten people in all, and so he determined to know Mr. Austin Dobson and myself, "to add a little new blood," as he put it. For my part, I was too raw and inexperienced to appreciate the distinction of his choice, but not too dull to value the soft goings and comings of this moth-like man, so hushed and faded, like a delicate withered leaf, so mysterious, so profoundly learned, so acutely sensitive that an inflection in the voice seemed to chill him like a cold wind, so refined that with an ardent thought the complexion of his intellect seemed to flush like the cheek of a girl.

He was forty at that time, but looked older. Those who have seen him in these last years recall a finer presence, a more "striking" personality. Of late he carried upon his bending shoulders a veritable *tête de roi en exil;* he reminded us, towards the end, of one of the fallen brethren of Hyperion. But in 1875, in his unobtrusive dress, with his timid, fluttering manner, there was nothing at all impressive in the outer guise of him. He seemed to melt into the twilight of a corner, to succeed, as far as a mortal can, in being invisible. This evasive ghost, in a loose snuff-coloured coat, would always be the first person in the room to be overlooked by a superficial observer. It was in a *tête-à-tête* across the corner of the mahogany, under a lamplight that emphasised the noble modelling of the forehead, and lighted up the pale azure eyes, that a companion saw what manner of man he was dealing with, and half-divined, perhaps, the beauty and wisdom of this unique and astonishing mind. It was an education to be permitted to listen to him then, to receive his slight and intermittent confidences, to pour out, with the inconsiderate egotism of youth, one's own hopes and failures, to feel this infinitely refined and sensitive spirit benignantly concentrated on one's prentice efforts, which seemed to grow a little riper and more dignified by the mere benediction of that smile. His intellect, in my opinion, was a singularly healthy one, and, therefore, in its almost preternatural quickness and many-sidedness, calculated to help and stimulate the minds of others. It did not guide or command, it simply radiated light around the steps of a friend. The radiance was sometimes faint, but it was exquisite, and it seemed omnipresent.

Yet it is unquestionable that to most of those who saw Lord De Tabley casually, his manner gave the impression more of hypochondria than of health. That excessive sensitiveness of his, which shrank from the slightest impact of what was, or what even faintly seemed to be, unsympathetic, could but produce on the superficial observer an idea of want of self-command. To pretend that the equilibrium of his spirit was not disturbed would be idle; the turmoil of his nerves was written on those fierce and timid eyes of his. But it is only right now to say, and to say with insistence, that it was no indulgence of eccentricity, no wilful melancholy, that made him so quivering and shrinking a soul. He had suffered from troubles such as now may well be buried in his grave, sorrows that beset him from his youth up, disappointments and disillusions that dogged him to the very close of his career, and made death itself almost welcome to him, although he loved life so well. He was one who, like Gray, "never spoke out," and only those who knew him best could divine what the foxes were that gnawed the breast under the cloak. Very few human beings are pursued from the beginning of life to its close with so many distracting griefs and perplexities, such a combination of misfortunes and wearing annoyances, as this gentle-hearted poet, who grew, at last, so harried by the implacable ingenuity of his destiny that a movement or a word would awaken his fatalistic alarm.

The knowledge of this should now account for a good deal that puzzled and even grieved his friends. Moral and physical suffering had rendered the epidermis of his character so excessively thin that the merest trifle pained him; he was like those unfortunate persons who are born without a scarf-skin, on whom the pressure of a twig or the grip of a hand brings blood. This sensitiveness was pitiable, and the results of it even a little blameworthy, since, if they entailed wretchedness on himself, they caused needless pain to those who truly loved him. I doubt if any friend, however tactful in self-abnegation, got through many years of Lord De Tabley's intimacy without an electric storm. His imagination aided his ingenuity in self-torture, and conjured up monsters of malignity, spectres that strode across the path of friendship and rendered it impassable. But his tempestuous heat was not greater than his placability, and those who had not patience to wait the return of his kinder feelings can scarcely have been worthy of them.

He lived for friendship—poetry and his friends were the two lode-stars of his life. Yet he cultivated his intimates oddly. He sometimes reminded me of a bird-fancier with all his pets in separate cages; he attended to each of them in turn, but he did not choose that they should mix in a general social aviary. He was not unwilling to meet the acquaintances of his friends, but he did not care to bring his intimates much into contact with one another. Probably the number of these last was greater than any one of them was accustomed to realise. At the head of them all, I think, stood Sir Mountstuart Grant Duff; not far behind, Sir A. W. Franks. Besides these companions of his youth, he cultivated among the friends of his middle life, Sir Henry Howorth, Mr. W. T. Thiselton-Dyer, and others, each linked with him by a combination of tastes—antiquarianism, numismatics, zoology, horticulture, some pursuit which made the woof of a texture in which personal sympathy was the warp. But he lived among the dead, and to these his attitude was much the same as that of a priest in the shrine of his vanished deities. To him the unseen faces were often more real than the living ones.

The side on which I was most capable of appreciating

Lord de Tabley's gifts as a collector was the bibliographical. If I am anything of a connoisseur in this direction, I owe it to his training. His zeal in the amassing of early editions of the English poets was extreme; he was one of those who think nothing of hanging about a book-shop at six in the morning, waiting for the shutters to be taken down. But his zeal was eminently according to knowledge. He valued his first edition for the text's sake, not for the bare fact of rarity. Every book he bought he read, and with a critical gusto. A little anecdote may illustrate his spirit as a collector. In 1877 he secured, by a happy accident, a copy of Milton's *Poems* of 1645, a book which he had never met with before. Too eager to wait for the post, he sent a messenger round to my house with a note to announce not merely the joyful fact, but—this is the interesting point—a discovery he had made in the volume, namely, that the line in the "Nativity Ode," which in all later editions has run,

Orb'd in a rainbow, and like glories wearing,

originally stood,

The enamell'd arras of the rainbow wearing,

"which," as he said, "is a grand mouthful of sound, and ever so much better than the weak 'like glories.'"

I shall not forget, when dining alone with him once at Onslow Square, noticing that at the beginning of the meal he was strangely distraught. At length, the post came, and Warren (as he then was) tore open one envelope wildly; he read the first words, and sank back faint in his chair, hiding his eyes with his hands. I was convinced that some terrible calamity had happened to him, but it was only that he had secured a first edition of Shelley's *Alastor* at a country auction, and—*la joie faisait peur!* For some of his little, rare seventeenth-century volumes, he had an almost petulant affection. He has celebrated in beautiful verse his copy of Suckling's *Fragmenta Aurea;* and perhaps I may be allowed to tell one more bibliomaniac story. On a certain occasion when I was at his house, Robert Browning and Frederick Locker being the other guests, Warren had put on the table his latest prize, a copy of Sir William Davenant's *Madagascar* of 1638. Browning presently got hold of the little book, and began reading passages aloud, making fun of the poetry (which, indeed, is pretty bad) with "Listen, now, to this," and "Here's a fine conceit." Warren bore it for a little while, and then he very gently took the volume out of Browning's hands, and hid it away. "Oh!" he explained to me afterwards, "I could not allow him to *patronise* Davenant."

A particular favourite with him was Quarles, as combining the metaphysical poet with the emblematist. He had a curious theory that the influence, not only of Quarles, but of Alciati, could be traced in the designs of Blake, another special object of his study. Before I leave bibliography I am tempted to quote a passage from one of De Tabley's delightful letters, now nearly twenty years old:

"I have been cheered up by buying to-day a copy of

Henry Lawes' *Ayres for the Theorbo; or, Bas Viol*, 1653, with some Herrick and Lovelace pieces set. Also a Spenser of 1610, the first collected Folio, with nice little plates to the *Shepherd's Calendar*—one each month. I must tell you, for very idiocy—I had the most vivid dream last night that you and I were cardinals, turning over books in the Vatican Library. I remember the look of my own red stockings. We were both in cardinal red from top to toe. I felt quite pleased to be so smart, but your robes seemed better made. How infinitely absurd! But so vivid. A certain room I remembered in the Vatican came back fresh, and the exact dress of the old creatures I saw at the Council (in 1869)."

Bibliography and the ardour of the collector led Warren by degrees into a department where he was destined to exercise a considerable influence. His love of books extended to a study of those marks of ownership which are known as *ex-libris*, and in 1880 he published *A Guide to the Study of Book-plates*, a handsomely illustrated volume which has been the pioneer of many interesting works, and of a whole society of students and annotators. He was led to the historical study of the book-plate by his love of heraldry, which was to be traced, too, in more than one passage of his poetry. I cannot recollect that his enthusiasm for books extended to bindings. His own library, of which it was his intention to prepare a privately printed catalogue—a project which his premature death has frustrated—was not conspicuous bibliopegically. He belonged to the class of bibliophiles whose books lie strewn over sofas and armchairs, instead of being ranged in cases like jewels. His servant, I recollect his telling me, became so incensed with his books that he grew to regard them as personal enemies, and when, about 1879, Warren proposed to move from Onslow Square, this man snorted with the joy of battle, and said, "At last I'll be even with them dummed books."

He was writing poetry to the last, and I think, from what he very lately wrote to me, that a volume of MS. verses will be found almost ready for the press. It was a great pleasure to him to know that many of his fellow-craftsmen were now eager to receive his work. Mr. Austin Dobson had always been an admirer, and one of the latest tributes which cheered De Tabley was a copy of verses from this friend of twenty years, which I have the privilege of printing here for the first time:

> *Still may the Muses foster thee, O Friend,*
>   *Who, while the vacant quidnuncs stand at gaze,*
> *Wondering what Prophet next the Fates will send,*
>   *Still tread'st the ancient ways;*
>
> *Still climb'st the clear-cold altitudes of Song,*
>   *Or, lingering " by the shore of old Romance,"*
> *Heed'st not the vogue, how little or how long,*
>   *Of marvels made in France.*
>
> *Still to the summits may thy face be set;*
>   *And long may we, that heard thy morning rhyme,*
> *Hang on thy mid-day music, nor forget*
>   *In the hushed even-time!*

Mr. Theodore Watts, too—whose touching and picturesque anecdotes in the *Athenæum* of November 30 are of real value in forming an impression of Lord De Tabley's character—was a constant and judicious encourager of his art.

In those three latest years of his partial reappearance in the world of letters, Lord De Tabley has rejoiced many of his old friends by a renewal of the early delightful relations. He has formed new friendships, too, among those who will remember his noble head and gentle, stately manners when we older ones have joined him. He appreciated the company of several members of the new school of poets, and especially that of Mr. William Watson, Mr. John Davidson, and Mr. Arthur Christopher Benson. The last named, I think, in particular, enjoyed a greater intimacy with him than any other man who is now less than thirty-five years of age. There has been so much of the elder generation, then, in this little memoir, that I prefer to close with a few words written to me by this latest friend when the death was announced—words which Mr. Benson kindly permits me to print:

"Lord de Tabley always struck me as being a curious instance of the irony of destiny—a man with so many sources of pleasure and influence open to him—his love of literature, his mastery of style, his conversational charm, his social position, his affectionate nature—yet bearing always about with him a curious attitude of resignation and disappointment, as though life were, on the whole, a sad business, and, for the sake of courtesy and decency, the less said about it the better. I must repeat the word 'courtesy,' for, like a subtle fragrance, it interpenetrated all he did or said. It seemed the natural aroma of an exquisitely sensitive, delicate, and considerate spirit. There was something archaic, almost, one might say, hierarchical, about his head, with its long, rippled, grey hair, the transparent pallor of complexion, the piercing eye. He dressed with the same severity, and, though I never heard him speak of religion, there was about him a certain monastic stateliness of air which one sees most frequently in those who combine worldly position with the possession of a tranquillising faith. He contrived to inspire affection to a singular extent. Perhaps there was a certain pathos about his life and the strange contradictions it contained, but I think there was also in him a deep need of affection, and, in spite of his determined effort after courage and calm, an intimate despair of gaining the encouragement of others."

This is beautifully said, I think, and delicately felt, yet, like all our attempts to analyse the fugitive charm of this extraordinary being, it leaves the memory unsatisfied.

1896

TORU DUTT

Toru Dutt

IF Toru Dutt were alive, she would still (in 1882) be younger than any recognised European writer, and yet her fame, which is already considerable, has been entirely posthumous. Within the brief space of four years which now divides us from the date of her decease, her genius has been revealed to the world under many phases, and has been recognised in France and England. Her name, at least, is no longer unfamiliar in the ear of any well-read man or woman. But at the hour of her death she had published but one book, and that book had found but two reviewers in Europe. One of these, M. André Theuriet, the well-known poet and novelist, gave the *Sheaf gleaned in French Fields* adequate praise in the *Revue des Deux Mondes;* but the other, the writer of the present notice, has a melancholy satisfaction in having been a little earlier still in sounding the only note of welcome which reached the dying poetess from England.

It was while Professor W. Minto was editor of the *Examiner*, that one day in August, 1876, in the very heart of the dead season for books, I happened to be in the office of that newspaper, and was upbraiding the whole body of publishers for issuing no books worth reviewing. At that moment the postman brought in a thin and sallow packet with a wonderful Indian postmark on it, and containing a most unattractive orange pamphlet of verse, printed at Bhowanipore, and entitled "*A Sheaf gleaned in French Fields*, by Toru Dutt." This shabby little book of some two hundred pages, without preface or introduction, seemed specially destined by its particular providence to find its way hastily into the waste-paper basket. I remember that Mr. Minto thrust it into my unwilling hands, and said "There! see whether you can't make something of that." A hopeless volume it seemed, with its queer type, published at Bhowanipore, printed at the Saptahiksambad Press! But when at last I took it out of my pocket, what was my surprise and almost rapture to open at such verse as this:

> *Still barred thy doors!   The far-east glows,*
> *The morning wind blows fresh and free.*
> *Should not the hour that wakes the rose*
> *Awaken also thee?*
>
> *All look for thee, Love, Light, and Song—*
> *Light in the sky deep red above,*
> *Song, in the lark of pinions strong,*
> *And in my heart, true Love.*
>
> *Apart we miss our nature's goal,*
> *Why strive to cheat our destinies?*
> *Was not my love made for thy soul?*
> *Thy beauty for mine eyes?*

No longer sleep,
 Oh, listen now!
I wait and weep,
 But where art thou!

When poetry is as good as this it does not much matter whether Rouveyre prints it upon Whatman paper, or whether it steals to light in blurred type from some press in Bhowanipore.

Toru Dutt was the youngest of the three children of a high-caste Hindu couple in Bengal. Her father, who survived them all, the Baboo Govin Chunder Dutt, was himself distinguished among his countrymen for the width of his views and the vigour of his intelligence. His only son, Abju, died in 1865, at the age of fourteen, and left his two younger sisters to console their parents. Aru, the elder daughter, born in 1854, was eighteen months senior to Toru, the subject of this memoir, who was born in Calcutta on the 4th of March, 1856. With the exception of one year's visit to Bombay, the childhood of these girls was spent in Calcutta, at their father's garden-house. In a poem I printed for the first time, Toru refers to the scene of her earliest memories, the circling wilderness of foliage, the shining tank with the round leaves of the lilies, the murmuring dusk under the vast branches of the central casuarina-tree. Here, in a mystical retirement more irksome to an European in fancy than to an Oriental in reality, the brain of this wonderful child was moulded. She was pure Hindu, full of the typical qualities of her race and blood, and preserving to the last her appreciation of the poetic side of her ancient religion, though faith itself in Vishnu and Siva had been cast aside with childish things and been replaced by a purer faith. Her mother fed her imagination with the old songs and legends of their people, stories which it was the last labour of her life to weave into English verse; but it would seem that the marvellous faculties of Toru's mind still slumbered, when, in her thirteenth year, her father decided to take his daughters to Europe to learn English and French. To the end of her days Toru was a better French than English scholar. She loved France best, she knew its literature best, she wrote its language with more perfect elegance. The Dutts arrived in Europe at the close of 1869, and the girls went to school, for the first and last time, at a French pension. They did not remain there very many months; their father took them to Italy and England with him, and finally they attended for a short time, but with great zeal and application, the lectures for women at Cambridge. In November, 1873, they went back again to Bengal, and the four remaining years of Toru's life were spent in the old garden-house at Calcutta, in a feverish dream of intellectual effort and imaginative production. When we consider what she achieved in these forty-five months of seclusion, it is impossible to wonder that the frail and hectic body succumbed under so excessive a strain.

She brought with her from Europe a store of knowledge that would have sufficed to make an English or French girl seem learned, but which in her case was simply miraculous. Immediately on her return she began to study Sanskrit with the same intense application which she gave to all her work, and mastering the language with extraordinary swiftness, she plunged into its mysterious literature. But she was born to write, and despairing of an audience in her own language, she began to adopt ours as a medium for her thought. Her first essay, published when she was eighteen, was a monograph in the *Bengal Magazine*, on Leconte de Lisle, a writer with whom she had a sympathy which is very easy to comprehend. The austere poet of *La Mort de Valmiki* was, obviously, a figure to whom the poet of *Sindhu* must needs be attracted on approaching European literature. This study, which was illustrated by translations into English verse, was followed by another on Joséphin Soulary, in whom she saw more than her maturer judgment might have justified.

There is something very interesting and now, alas! still more pathetic in these sturdy and workmanlike essays in unaided criticism. Still more solitary her work became, in July, 1874, when her only sister, Aru, died, at the age of twenty. She seems to have been no less amiable than her sister, and if gifted with less originality and a less forcible ambition, to have been finely accomplished. Both sisters were well-trained musicians, with full contralto voices, and Aru had a faculty for design which promised well. The romance of *Mlle. D'Arvers* was originally projected for Aru to illustrate, but no page of this book did Aru ever see.

In 1876, as we have seen, appeared that obscure first volume at Bhowanipore. The *Sheaf gleaned in French Fields* is certainly the most imperfect of Toru's writings, but it is not the least interesting. It is a wonderful mixture of strength and weakness, of genius overriding great obstacles and of talent succumbing to ignorance and inexperience. That it should have been performed at all is so extraordinary that we forget to be surprised at its inequality. The English verse is sometimes exquisite; at other times the rules of our prosody are absolutely ignored, and it is obvious that the Hindu poetess was chanting to herself a music that is discord in an English ear. The notes are no less curious, and to a stranger no less bewildering. Nothing could be more naïve than the writer's ignorance at some points, or more startling than her learning at others.

On the whole, the attainment of the book was simply astounding. It consisted of a selection of translations from nearly one hundred French poets, chosen by the poetess herself on a principle of her own which gradually dawned upon the careful reader. She eschewed the Classicist writers as though they had never existed. For her André Chenier was the next name in chronological order after Du Bartas. Occasionally she showed a profundity of research that would have done no discredit to Mr. Saintsbury or *le doux Assellineau*. She was ready to pronounce an opinion on Napol le Pyrénéan or to detect a plagiarism in Baudelaire. But she thought that Alexander Smith was still alive, and she was curiously vague about the career of

Sainte Beuve. This inequality of equipment was a thing inevitable to her isolation, and hardly worth recording, except to show how laborious her mind was, and how quick to make the best of small resources.

We have already seen that the *Sheaf gleaned in French Fields* attracted the very minimum of attention in England. In France it was talked about a little more. M. Garcin de Tassy, the famous Orientalist, who scarcely survived Toru by twelve months, spoke of it to Mlle. Clarisse Bader, author of a somewhat remarkable book on the position of women in ancient Indian society. Almost simultaneously this volume fell into the hands of Toru, and she was moved to translate it into English, for the use of Hindus less instructed than herself. In January, 1877, she accordingly wrote to Mlle. Bader requesting her authorisation, and received a prompt and kind reply. On the 18th of March Toru wrote again to this, her solitary correspondent in the world of European literature, and her letter, which has been preserved, shows that she had already descended into the valley of the shadow of death:

"Ma constitution n'est pas forte; j'ai contracté une toux opiniâtre, il y a plus de deux ans, qui ne me quitte point. Cependant j'espère mettre la main à l'œuvre bientôt. Je ne peux dire, mademoiselle, combien votre affection—car vous les aimez, votre livre et votre lettre en témoignent assez—pour mes compatriotes et mon pays me touche; et je suis fière de pouvoir le dire que les héroïnes de nos grandes épopées sont dignes de tout honneur et de tout amour. Y a-ti-il d'héroïne plus touchante, plus aimable que Sîta ? Je ne le crois pas. *Quand j'entends ma mère chanter, le soir, les vieux chants de notre pays, je pleure presque toujours.* La plainte de Sita, quand, bannie pour la séconde fois, elle erre dans la vaste forêt, seule, le désespoir et l'effroi dans l'âme, est si pathétique qu'il n'y a personne, je crois, qui puisse l'entendre sans verser des larmes. Je vous envois sous ce pli deux petites traductions du Sanscrit, cette belle langue antique. Malheureusement j'ai été obligée de faire cesser mes traductions de Sanscrit, il y a six mois. Ma santé ne me permet pas de les continuer."

These simple and pathetic words, in which the dying poetess pours out her heart to the one friend she had, and that one gained too late, seem as touching and as beautiful as any strain of Marceline Valmore's immortal verse. In English poetry I do not remember anything that exactly parallels their resigned melancholy. Before the month of March was over, Toru had taken to her bed. Unable to write, she continued to read, strewing her sick room with the latest European books, and entering with interest into the questions raised by the Société Asiatique of Paris in its printed *Transactions*. On the 30th of July she wrote her last letter to Mlle. Clarisse Bader, and a month later, on the 30th of August, 1877, at the age of twenty-one years, six months, and twenty-six days, she breathed her last in her father's house in Maniktollah Street, Calcutta.

In the first distraction of grief it seemed as though

her unequalled promise had been entirely blighted, and as though she would be remembered only by her single book. But as her father examined her papers, one completed work after another revealed itself. First a selection from the sonnets of the Comte de Grammont, translated into English, turned up, and was printed in a Calcutta magazine; then some fragments of an English story, which was printed in another Calcutta magazine. Much more important, however, than any of these was a complete romance, written in French, being the identical story for which her sister Aru had proposed to make the illustrations. In the meantime Toru was no sooner dead than she began to be famous. In May, 1878, there appeared a second edition of the *Sheaf gleaned in French Fields*, with a touching sketch of her death, by her father; and in 1879 was published, under the editorial care of Mlle. Clarisse Bader, the romance of *Le Journal de Mlle. D'Arvers*, forming a handsome volume of 259 pages. This book, begun as it appears before the family returned from Europe, and finished nobody knows when, is an attempt to describe scenes from modern French society, but it is less interesting as an experiment of the fancy, than as a revelation of the mind of a young Hindu woman of genius. The story is simple, clearly told, and interesting; the studies of character have nothing French about them, but they are full of vigour and originality. The description of the hero is most characteristically Indian:

"Il est beau en effet. Sa taille est haute, mais

quelques-uns la trouveraient mince ; sa chevelure noire est bouclée et tombe jusqu'à la nuque ; ses yeux noirs sont profonds et bien fendus ; le front est noble ; la lèvre supérieure, couverte par une moustache naissante et noire, est parfaitement modelée ; son menton a quelque chose de sévère ; son teint est d'un blanc presque féminin, ce qui dénote sa haute naissance."

In this description we seem to recognise some Surya or Soma of Hindu mythology, and the final touch, meaningless as applied to an European, reminds us that in India whiteness of skin has always been a sign of aristocratic birth, from the days when it originally distinguished the conquering Aryas from the indigenous race of the Dasyous.

As a literary composition *Mlle. D'Arvers* deserves considerable commendation. It deals with the ungovernable passion of two brothers for one placid and beautiful girl, a passion which leads to fratricide and madness. That it is a very melancholy and tragical story is obvious from this brief suggestion of its contents, but it is remarkable for coherence and self-restraint no less than for vigour of treatment. Toru Dutt never sinks to melodrama in the course of her extraordinary tale, and the wonder is that she is not more often fantastic and unreal.

But I believe that the original English poems, which I presented to the public for the first time in 1882, will be ultimately found to constitute Tora's chief legacy to posterity. These ballads form the last and most matured of her writings, and were left so far fragmentary at her death that the fourth and fifth in her projected series of nine were not to be discovered in any form among her papers. It is probable that she had not even commenced them. Her father, therefore, to give a certain continuity to the series, filled up these blanks with two stories from the *Vishnupurana* which originally appeared respectively in the *Calcutta Review* and in the *Bengal Magazine*. These are interesting, but a little rude in form, and they have not the same peculiar value as the rhymed octo-syllabic ballads. In these last we see Toru no longer attempting vainly, though heroically, to compete with European literature on its own ground, but turning to the legends of her own race and country for inspiration. No modern Oriental has given us so strange an insight into the conscience of the Asiatic as is presented in the stories of "Prehlad" and of "Savitri," or so quaint a piece of religious fancy as the ballad of "Jogadhya Uma." The poetess seems in these verses to be chanting to herself those songs of her mother's race to which she always turned with tears of pleasure. They breathe a Vedic solemnity and simplicity of temper, and are singularly devoid of that littleness and frivolity which seem, if I may judge by a slight experience, to be the bane of modern Indian literature.

As to the merely technical character of the poems, it may be suggested that in spite of much in them that is rough and inchoate, they show that Toru was advancing in her mastery of English verse. Such a stanza as this, selected out of many no less skilful

o

could hardly be recognised as the work of one by whom the language was a late acquirement:

> *What glorious trees! The sombre saul,*
>   *On which the eye delights to rest—*
> *The betel-nut, a pillar tall,*
>   *With feathery branches for a crest—*
> *The light-leaved tamarind spreading wide—*
>   *The pale faint-scented bitter neem,*
> *The seemul, gorgeous as a bride,*
>   *With flowers that have the ruby's gleam.*

In other passages, of course, the text reads like a translation from some stirring ballad, and we feel that it gives but a faint and discordant echo of the music welling in Toru's brain. For it must frankly be confessed that in the brief May-day of her existence she had not time to master our language as Blanco White did, or as Chamisso mastered German. To the end of her days, fluent and graceful as she was, she was not entirely conversant with English, especially with the colloquial character of modern speech. Often a very fine thought is spoiled for hypercritical ears by the queer turn of expression which she has innocently given to it. These faults are found to a much smaller degree in her miscellaneous poems. Her sonnets, printed in 1882, seem to me to be of great beauty, and her longer piece entitled "Our Casuarina Tree," needs no apology for its rich and mellifluous numbers:

> *Like a huge python, winding round and round*
>   *The rugged trunk, indented deep with scars,*

Up to its very summit near the stars,
A creeper climbs, in whose embraces bound
   No other tree could live.   But gallantly
The giant wears the scarf, and flowers are hung
In crimson clusters all the boughs among,
   Whereon all day are gathered bird and bee;
And oft at nights the garden overflows
With one sweet song that seems to have no close,
Sung darkling from our tree, while men repose.

When first my casement is wide open thrown
   At dawn, my eyes delighted on it rest;
   Sometimes—and most in winter—on its crest
A grey baboon sits statue-like alone
   Watching the sunrise; while on lower boughs
His puny offspring leap about and play;
And far and near kokilas hail the day;
   And to their pastures wend our sleepy cows;
And in the shadow, on the broad tank cast
By that hoar tree, so beautiful and vast,
The water-lilies spring, like snow enmassed.

   *   *   *   *

Therefore I fain would consecrate a lay
   Unto thy honour, Tree, beloved of those
   Who now in blessed sleep, for aye, repose;
Dearer than life to me, alas! were they!
   Mays't thou be numbered when my days are done
With deathless Trees—like those in Borrowdale,
Under whose awful branches lingered pale
   "Fear, trembling Hope, and Death, the skeleton,
And Time, the shadow;" and though weak the verse
That would thy beauty fain, oh fain rehearse,
May Love defend thee from Oblivion's curse.

It is difficult to exaggerate when we try to estimate what we have lost in the premature death of Toru Dutt. Literature has no honours which need have been beyond the grasp of a girl who before the age of twenty-one, and in languages separated from her own by so deep a chasm, had produced so much of lasting worth. And her courage and fortitude were worthy of her intelligence. Among "last words" of celebrated people, that which her father has recorded, "It is only the physical pain that makes me cry," is not the least remarkable, or the least significant of strong character. It was to a native of our island, and to one ten years senior to Toru, to whom it was said, in words more appropriate, surely, to her than to Oldham,

> *Thy generous fruits, though gathered ere their prime,*
> *Still showed a quickness, and maturing time*
> *But mellows what we write to the dull sweets of Rime.*

That mellow sweetness was all that Toru lacked to perfect her as an English poet, and of no other Oriental who has ever lived can the same be said. When the history of the literature of our country comes to be written, there is sure to be a page in it dedicated to this fragile exotic blossom of song.

1882.

M. JOSÉ-MARIA DE HEREDIA

M. José-Maria de Heredia

THAT M. Zola will, in due course of time, push his way into the Institute, and become authorised to wear the greenest of palm-shoots, is doubtless inevitable, nor have I any objection to offer. But, for the life of me, I cannot understand why, all of a sudden, the English press has become so exceedingly anxious to see this little affair of literary honour arranged. The reception given in this country to the latest election at the French Academy was comically unaccountable. Why has it abruptly become necessary that a dignified, ancient and scholarly body should open its doors to the author of *Pot-Bouille*, knocking so noisily upon them with reverberations of congenial brass? The spirit of modern democracy, we are told, demands that the possessor of such swarms of editions should be an Academician, and when he is kept waiting for a little while (it will only be for a little while—calm yourself, beating heart of the democracy!), shouts out that the Academy is decrepit and obsolete, and must be swept off the face of the earth. Permit the great M. Zola to kick his heels in the cold, while you let in a gentleman who has only written a few sonnets? Shameful nepotism, shocking decrepitude! The fact is, it is time that we should cease to laugh at the French for their affection for the Russians. We are making ourselves still more ridiculous by our preposterous solicitude for M. Zola.

With those who regret that our Tudor kings started no such literary order of merit as the French Academy, I do not greatly sympathise, and still less with those who recommend the creation to-day of a brand-new institution of the kind. Still, looking across the water to France, I do see that there are functions which so ancient a body as that which sits in the Mazarine Palace can, and does, exercise with high advantage to the public. The inclusion of M. Zola, though not necessarily foreign to the aim of such a body, does eminently strike me as not being one of those functions. He has his editions, his wealth, and his fame, the tributes of the democracy. But what a set of men in the position of the thirty-nine electing Academicians, raised above fear of public displeasure, made a law unto themselves, can do is to protect and reward distinguished and delicate talent, of a very original order, which does not appeal to the loud public. The French Academy can afford to wave aside the novelist who comes with all his drums and trumpets, and a flushed cohort of camp followers shouting in his wake, and can say to the poet who does not strive nor cry, who cultivates a noble art in austerity, "Be pleased, sir, to join our company; there will be room for this popular gentleman by-and-by." That the French Academy has done this by electing M. de Heredia to the seat vacated by the death of M. de Mazade seems to me an unusually effective exercise of a wholesome and valuable privilege.

Wholesome, because it is necessary for the health of the intellectual life in this crowded and degenerated atmosphere of ours to be encouraged to climb the heights and taste the colder air; valuable, because it rewards a decent and dignified ambition in a mode that is more direct than any other which is open to the literary world of to-day. The election of M. de Heredia to the French Academy is an important and critical event in the imaginative history of our time, because it is a public statement of the value set by a group of men of high and yet dissimilar intellectual character on work that is superlatively well done, on the work of a craftsman who has not allowed himself to be hurried or disturbed by any pressure from without, who has not cared to move an inch from his path to please the many or the few, who has spent half a lifetime in the pursuit of a splendid perfection, a faultless magnificence in concentrated and chiselled verse. It is the occasional appearance, in our slipshod world, of artists so consummate as M. de Heredia that keeps poetry from being degraded to a mere shabby volubility. *Data Romanis venia est indigna poetis*, and the only way in which the standard can be raised to its normal severity is by occasional reference to those writers who live up to the most rigid executive ideal. It is as a jeweller in verse, a poetical artificer of the very highest merit that M. de Heredia has earned for himself the applause of the Institute. We hear a great deal of the experimentalists who are

trying to dissolve and deliquesce the prosody of France.
Let us acquaint ourselves, in justice, with the man who
has done most during the last ten years to keep it as
hard and as brilliant as fine bronze.

I

So far as I am aware, no biography or even biographical sketch of M. de Heredia has ever been published. His is the proud and self-contained nature, no doubt, that shrinks from publicity as from a familiar touch. The details I give below are the mosaic of an affectionate though secret admirer, who has carefully stored up, through more than twenty years, every scrap of information which has fallen in his way respecting a poet whose genius is intimately sympathetic to him.

José-Maria de Heredia is a Cuban by birth. He traces his ancestry direct from one of the first conquerors of the New World. He is of the bluest blood of Spanish colonial aristocracy. He tells me that he is the direct descendant of that Adelantado don Pedro de Heredia, who came to America in the company of the second Admiral Diego Columbus, and who founded Cartagena in the West Indies. To this ancestor he has alluded in several of his poems. In the extreme south of the island, above the bay and city of Santiago de Cuba, in a glen of the Sierra Maestra looking over the ocean southward towards Jamaica, he was born on the 22nd of November, 1842. His home was the coffee plantation of La Fortuna, one of the last possessions of a noble but impoverished family. On the mother's side, however, he is of French origin. At the age of eight he was brought to Paris, and received his earliest education at the College of St. Vincent at Senlis. Nine years in Europe made a Frenchman of him, but at seventeen he went back to Cuba. For a year he worked at the University of Havannah; then, about 1860, finally returned to France, and took up his studies in the law. He tells me that he sadly neglected them, and then, with greater zest, entered the École des Chartes. In Cuba, I am told, they reproach him with having robbed Spain of a Spanish poet; but, in truth, M. de Heredia is scarcely more a Spaniard than Rossetti was an Italian.

In 1862 he published his first verses in the then existing *Revue de Paris*, the far-away ancestor of MM. Darmesteter and Ganderax's new venture. I know not what these "first verses" were. But in 1866 he was one of the happy band of lyric boys who started the *Parnasse Contemporain*, that *Germ* of France. This anthology was brought out under the auspices and the patronage of M. Leconte de Lisle, whose influence over recent French poetry has been greater than that of any other person. Among the youthful Parnassians were almost all the men who have since that day come prominently to the front in poetical literature—Sully Prudhomme and François Coppée, Paul Verlaine and Catulle Mendès, Stéphane Mallarmé and Léon Dierx. Among them, and from the very first, the young Heredia distinguished himself by the severe ideal of his art, and by his disdain of the common tricks by which men rise. He remembered the blood of the founder of Cartagena.

In one of his delicious essays, M. Anatole France, himself a Parnassian, recalls the features of that happy time. He has a little vignette portrait of each of his old comrades, and here is what he says of the poet of *Les Trophées:*

"Alone, or almost alone, in our *cénacle*, M. José-Maria de Heredia, although defrauded of a great part of the treasure of his ancestors, the *conquistadores*, affected the young gentleman of fashion, and smoked excellent cigars. His neckties were as splendid as his sonnets. But it was of the sonnets alone that we were jealous; for we all disdained the gifts of fortune. We loved nothing but fame, and we wished that if we were famous it might be in a discreet and almost secret way."

Already, in this very early time, it was the magnificent precision of Heredia's sonnets which attracted the attention of his elders; and Théophile Gautier, that benevolent Olympian, exclaimed, on putting down the *Parnasse Contemporain*, "Heredia, I love you, because the name you bear is exotic and sonorous, and because you make verses that curl up at the ends like heraldic scallops."

The rest of the Parnassians, one after another, committed little volumes of independent verse, the first steps in so many active poetic careers. M. de Heredia alone remained aloof and impersonal, now and then dropping an impeccable sonnet into somebody else's nest. He was prominent in the second *Parnasse Contemporain*, that of 1869. My own first acquaintance with him was made in a volume of *Sonnets et Eaux-fortes*, published by Lemerre in 1869, and now extremely rare. I copied out, more than twenty years ago, from this expensive and unattainable work, a sonnet which appeared to me then, as it still appears, of a magnificent and refulgent perfection. This was *Les Conquérants*, now the first of a sequence of eight poems :

> *Comme un vol ae gerfauts hors du charnier natal,*
> *Fatigués de porter leurs misères hautaines,*
> *De Palos de Moguer, routiers et capitaines*
> *Partaient, ivres d'un rêve héroïque et brutal.*
>
> *Ils allaient conquérir le fabuleux métal*
> *Que Cipango mûrit dans ses mines lointaines,*
> *Et les vents alizés inclinaient leurs antennes*
> *Aux bords mystérieux du monde Occidental.*
>
> *Chaque soir, espérant des lendemains épiques,*
> *L'azur phosphorescent de la mer des Tropiques*
> *Enchantait leur sommeil d'un mirage doré ;*
>
> *Ou penchés à l'avant des blanches caravelles,*
> *Ils regardaient monter en un ciel ignoré*
> *Du fond de l'Océan des étoiles nouvelles.*

A little later, in the charming *Le Livre des Sonnets* edited by Charles Asselineau, other specimens came to light, and under the same mysterious conditions. It became, at last, a sort of collector's joy to watch the newspapers and reviews for stray sonnets of Heredia. Once there came, I forget where, a batch of no fewer than twenty-five at once, an event only to be paralleled, as a fact of exciting poetical significance, with the publication of Rossetti's *House of Life* in the *Fortnightly Review* for 1869. Those were days when a man might trudge forth from his house at the morning hour and meet angels in the street. "A happy time that was," as Wordsworth says, "triumphant looks Were then the common language of all eyes." I hope the young poetical fellows nowadays enjoy themselves with as much gaiety as we did in our implacable fanaticism for verse; but I fancy that the incessant paragraph and the newspaper column, avid of information, must lessen their pleasures. Half of ours lay in our remoteness and our concentrated narrowness of interest.

Much has changed since then, both in London and Paris. The whole face of fashion has altered; the most famous names have become part of the heritage of history; youth, that made us what we were, and painted the dull places with such fiery colours, has passed. Only one thing remains absolutely unchanged, and that is the work of M. de Heredia. He reminds us of some craftsman in his studio, fingering his wax and hammering his thin plates of metal, while an army marches into his town, and is in turn driven out of it. He looks up, pale and dreamy, at the fall of afternoon, and has not heard an echo of the long day's battle.

The poet fashions his exquisite verses, one by one, and the world may look at them or not, as it pleases. Last summer, for the first time, M. de Heredia deigned to collect his scattered sonnets into a volume, *Les Trophées*,* a thirteenth edition of which had been printed before the close of 1893. If he waited long, until his life had passed its fiftieth year, before making an appeal to the great public, his reticence has received its reward. Rarely, indeed, has a book of poems so severe in form, making so stern a demand upon the gravity of the reader, achieved so substantial a success. And now, with the slender yellow volume of *Les Trophées* in his hand, he steps lightly up the staircase of the French Academy.

II

In all the literatures of Europe, the sonnet is preeminent in its pathetic and rhetorical forms. It is mainly subjective and Petrarchan. Any reader who turns over the leaves of a competent selection of English, or French, or Italian sonnets must be struck with the fact that in their large majority they express the secret sentiment or emotional experience of the soul, and that even where they seem to be descriptive, they deal mainly with the effect of external phenomena on the moods of the writer. No species of poetry is more confidential than the sonnet; none has been used, since its first

---

* *Les Trophées.* Par José-Maria de Heredia. Paris: Alphonse Lemerre, 1893.

invention, more persistently for the transmission of those secret thoughts which almost evade articulate expression. The innumerous sonnet-cycles of the Elizabethan age, from those of Shakespeare and Spenser downwards, were either pure exercises in Petrarchan amorosity, or they gave voice to an impossible emotion of which the direct utterance would have been indiscreet. The sonnets of Milton are louder in tone, and more impersonal; they represent, however, the element of pure and mellifluous eloquence rather than of detached poetical observation. The tone is no longer the whisper of a lover in pain, but although the sonneteer speaks from the rostrum, the appeal is always to his own experience and desires.

It is the same in French poetry. It would be difficult to collect out of the abundant Petrarchist literature of the sixteenth century a very small anthology of really objective sonnets. There are one or two of Ronsard's; there is the mysterious and beautiful octett of Amadis Jamyn's "Les ombres, les esprits, les idoles affreuses"; it would require some research to discover any other specimens into which the personal note of confession, entreaty, or rhetoric did not enter. When the revival of the sonnet began—in England more than a hundred years ago, in France more recently—the form was again captured for purely subjective uses. There are, of course, a few impersonal examples of Wordsworth and Keats. In our own day we have received some exquisite objective sonnets from Miss Christina Rossetti. But these are rare in England, and no less rare in France, where the difference between the two classes of sonnet, the introspective or philosophical, and the external or decorative, cannot be more clearly seen than by comparing the work of the two most eminent living sonneteers of France—M. Sully Prudhomme and M. de Heredia. If objective sonnets are rare in every collection, what must be our surprise to find that *Les Trophées* consists exclusively of this species of composition.

In the hands of M. de Heredia the sonnet takes a form of absolute regularity. The two rhymes of his octett (*ab-ba-ab-ba*) never change their positions; his sestett is permitted but two arrangements (*ccd-ede* or *ccd-eed*). He allows himself no licence of any kind; the frame is given to him, he has to fill it with absolute exactitude. This image of a picture in a gallery of paintings is one which it is difficult to dispense with in considering M. de Heredia's book. We find ourselves moving leisurely down a beautiful corridor, the walls of which are decorated, at regular intervals, with very highly finished panel-pictures, all of exactly the same size. It is now easy to understand why the public has been for so many years excluded from this gallery. The conscientious artist has not been willing that his work should be examined until it was complete, and the labour of completion has occupied half a lifetime. My eminent friend will forgive me, I think, if I quote in this connection a few words from a letter to myself: "Si je m'en suis tenu au sonnet," he says, "c'est que je trouve que dans sa forme à la fois mystique et mathématique, c'est le plus beau des poèmes à forme fixe et qu'il exige, par sa briéveté et sa difficulté, une conscience dans l'exécution et une concentration de la pensée qui ne peuvent qu'exciter et pousser à la perfection l'artiste digne de ce beau nom."

The first thing to be observed, in advancing along this rare and singular gallery, is that the paintings are by no means of an accidental arrangement or set in desultory sequence. The book is an attempt to present to the inward eye a regular series of carefully selected scenes from the imaginative history of the world. We shrink with horror from the notion of a *weltgeschichte* in quatorzains, and M. de Heredia, who is a master of the art of literary tact, would shudder sympathetically with us. What he designs is no more than a rapid descent of the ages, with here and there a momentary revelation of some highly suggestive and entertaining scene, or incident, or personage, rapidly given and as rapidly withdrawn, but seen for that moment with all the precision and effulgence possible, so that in the dimness of the grey past this one figure or incident may blaze out like a veritable luminary. For this purpose, everything needless, trifling or accidental, every triviality of expression, every superfluous phrase or image, must be rigidly suppressed. In so sudden and brief a revelation every touch must burn.

The central characteristic, then, of these splendid sonnets is their technical perfection. There is nothing loose or ungirt, nothing said vaguely because it would take time and labour to be precise. M. de Heredia opens his poem—for *Les Trophées* is really one poem in many sections—with a sonnet "L'Oubli." Oblivion, indeed, is the enemy he attacks. The temple on the Grecian promontory is ruined ; its goddesses of marble and its heroes of bronze lie broken and defaced under the dry and wind-blown grasses ; the sea at the foot of the headland moans and bewails the dead sirens of long ago. Not stone and not metal can defy oblivion ; the only truly immortal art, which no caprice of man or time can destroy, is verse. And so, in verse that shall be as like hammered bronze and carven marble as he can make it, the proudest of modern poets will try to save the fleeting world of beauty from decay.

Greece, first—since the savage and oriental parts of human development, which appeal so intimately to his master, M. Leconte de Lisle, have little or nothing to say to M. de Heredia. For him the symbol must be clear, brilliant, physical; he has no pleasure in mysticism or in the twilight of the intelligence. And this, indeed, must be confessed at once, that those who seek for tender notes and sunken lights, the vague sympathies of the soul, the melancholy music of experience, may go elsewhere ; the poet of *Les Trophées* is not for them. No man has less been touched by the malady of the age, no one is less attracted to the unknown and the distressful. M. de Heredia gazes straight at clear and beautiful things seen in a blaze of light ; almost every sonnet of his gives an impression of translucent air and brilliant sunshine. Alone, among French poets of to-day, the prevailing note of his work is joyous and heroic. Those ages of the world's history please him in which the symbolism of the imagination was sumptuous and noble. He possesses not a little of the grandiloquence of the race from which he sprang. His sonnets have the sound of a clarion, the human voice concentrated and uplifted by being blown through fine brass.

In the vestibule of his gallery of paintings we find six magnificent studies of Hercules and the Centaurs. This hero pleases him; he goes forth against lions, against centaurs (those emblems of hysterical human weakness), against perplexed and obscure hydras; he is strong and clear-headed, a lover of work strenuously fulfilled. So we find this story of Hercules told in a set of ringing sonnets, and we fancy ourselves opening the cabinet of a fifteenth-century Florentine medallist. With these and a few other exceptions, the Greek portion of *Les Trophées* may be passed over more rapidly than the rest. The sonnets dealing with the gods and the nymphs are somewhat cold; they are marble plaques in low relief, like fragments of a translation of Sophocles into sculpture. In this section of his book, the poet becomes most truly inspired, as it seems to me, when he deals with the legend of Pegasus, an animal for whom he nourishes a very tender regard. From several Perseus and Andromeda sonnets I select one, as it seems to me, of incomparable beauty:

Au milieu de l'écume arrêtant son essor,
Le Cavalier vainqueur du monstre et de Méduse,
Ruisselant d'une bave horrible où le sang fuse,
Emporte entre ses bras la vierge aux cheveux d'or.

Sur l'étalon divin, frère de Chrysaor,
Qui piaffe dans la mer et hennit et refuse,
Il a posé l'Amante éperdue et confuse
Qui lui rit et l'étreint et qui sanglote encor.

Il l'embrasse.   La houle enveloppe leur groupe.
Elle, d'un faible effort, ramène sur la croupe
Ses beaux pieds qu'en fuyant baise un flot vagabond;

Mais Pégase irrité par le fouet de la lame,
A l'appel du Héros s'enlevant d'un seul bond,
Bat le ciel ébloui de ses ailes de flamme.

As we decline to the latest schools of Greece, such successes as these are oftener repeated. In dealing with the sturdier pictures of antique life, I think that no critic can deny the superiority of M. Leconte de Lisle. The *Hyperion* of Keats is probably the only modern rival of the best portions of *Les Pöemes Antiques*. M. de Heredia cannot compress this vast music into the brief compass of his sonnet, nor do the exigencies of his form, complicated and concentrated as it is bound to be, permit these broader effects. But when it is not the tragedians whom he essays to follow, but when the lapidary art of the *Anthology* inspires him, when a runner, or a charioteer, the tomb of a grasshopper, or the prayer of shepherds to Pan, is the subject of one of his lucid and admirable sonnets, then he rises to the height of his genius. Nor, let it at once be said, with this sympathy for the civilised decline of a social order, does any littleness, any alexandrianism, any love of the quip or the conceit find place. All is on a restrained scale, but as pure and dignified as a relief by Donatello.

When the poet reaches Rome and the incursion of the Barbarians, the same characteristics are displayed. There is scarcely a touch of Virgil, nothing of Horace or Lucretius, but not a little of Catullus, and the very soul of Martial. Not merely, as may be seen by the comparison of the sonnet called "Lupercus" with the 118th epigram of the first book, is the very wine of the last-named poet poured, without loss of a drop spilled or diluted, into the chalice of the sonnet, but that is said which the manner of Martial suggests, yet, if it be not blasphemy to think so, better said. Will the shade of Desiré Nisard permit it to be whispered, for instance, that this is written as Martial would have written it, with modern knowledge, and a modern vocabulary to aid him?

AUX MONTAGNES DIVINES.

Geminus Servus
et pro suis conservis.

Glaciers bleus, pics de marbre et d'ardoise, granits,
Moraines dont le vent, du Néthou jusqu'à Bègle,
Arrache, brûle et tord le froment et le seigle,
Cols abrupts, lacs, forêts pleines d' ombre et de nids!

M. José-Maria de Heredia

Antres sourds, noirs vallons que les anciens bannis,
Plutôt que de ployer sous la servile règle,
Hantèrent avec l'ours, le loup, l'isard et l'aigle,
Précipices, torrents, gouffres, soyez bénis !

Ayant fui l'ergastule et le dur municipe,
L'esclave Geminus a dédié ce cippe
Aux Monts, gardiens sacrés de l'âpre liberté ;

Et sur ces sommets clairs où le silence vibre,
Dans l'air inviolable, immense et pur, jeté,
Je crois entendre encor le cri d'un homme libre !

In the section of his book entitled *The Middle Ages and the Renaissance*, M. de Heredia relinquishes himself to the pleasure of seizing little characteristic episodes, and treating them in the manner of a goldsmith. We find sonnets in which a picture of mediæval society is given with the rigidity, the clear, shadowless colour, and the transparency of a stained-glass window at Chartres or Le Mans; in which Balthazar, Melchior, and Gaspar, on their road to Bethany, cross a background of turquoise-coloured enamel; in which an epitaph is murmured over the extremely irreligious corpse of Hyacinthe, Seigneur de Maugiron, while tears furrow the rose-paint on the cheeks of Henri III.; in which a fading sheet of vellum, illuminated by Clovis Eve, is congratulated on having been caressed by the fingers of Diane de Poictiers. The censer, set with rubies, pearls, and beryls, over the chiselling of which Fray Juan de Segovia wore out his eyesight, this is more, one feels, to M. de Heredia than the ritual in which it is to be waved, and it is part of his sincerity that he apes no wide human sympathies in his conspectus of historical impressions.

But he is Cuban and a descendant of the Conquistadores; and he is lifted to more heroic flights, and a grander, because broader, conception of life, when, in a series of sonnets from which I have already quoted one, he celebrates the deeds of his colonial ancestors. He passes on to a lament over the decay of Spanish pride in the Americas, bewailing in one melodious sonnet after another the ruin of such dazzling hopes and the waste of prowess so magnificent. None of the poems of this section is more grandiose, nor any more interesting to us Englishmen, than the following on the decline of Cartagena;

A UNE VILLE MORTE.

Cartagena de Indias,
1532–1583–1697.

Morne Ville, jadis reine des Océans!
Aujourd'hui le requin poursuit en paix les scombres
Et le nuage errant allonge seul des ombres
Sur ta rade où roulaient les galions géants.

Depuis Drake et l'assaut des Anglais mécréants,
Tes murs désemparés croulent en noirs décombres,
Et, comme un glorieux collier de perles sombres,
Des boulets de Pointis montrent les trous béants.

Entre le ciel qui brûle et la mer qui moutonne,
Au somnolent soleil d'un midi monotone,
Tu songes, ô Guerrière, aux vieux Conquistadors ;

Et dans l'énervement des nuits chaudes et calmes,
Berçant ta gloire éteinte, ô Cité, tu t'endors
Sous les palmiers, au long frémissement des palmes.

We pass on to "The Orient and the Tropics." Here, again, we seem to catch something of the accent of M. Leconte de Lisle, to whom such figures as Kham and Hathor seem naturally dedicated. But in Japan M. de Heredia recovers the whole of his originality. He has succeeded, alone among poets of the West, in extracting from the art and the history of that miraculous archipelago its heroic and chivalrous splendour.

We are accustomed to an infusion of the sweeter tones, the more diaphanous graces of Japanese life into our poetry and our painting. What is novel, what M. de Heredia alone has given, is the mystery of the ancient aristocracy of Japan, with its fierce disregard of life, its savage sumptuousness, its extraordinary fulness of violent and vivid colour. He paints for us the Daimio on the field of battle, fluttering his satin-covered iron fan in front of his glaring eyes, while the lacquer coat-of-mail creaks on his panting bosom; or he gives us so strange a glimpse into the life of bygone Japan as is packed into this amazing sonnet:

LE SAMOURAI.

C'était un homme à deux sabres.

D'un doigt distrait frôlant la sonore bîva,
A travers les bambous tressés en fine latte,
Elle a vu, par la plage éblouissante et plate,
S'avancer le vainqueur que son amour rêva.

C'est lui. Sabres au flanc, l'éventail haut, il va.
La cordelière rouge et le gland écarlate
Coupent l'armure sombre, et, sur l'épaule, éclate
Le blason de Hizen ou de Tokungawa.

Ce beau guerrier vêtu de lames et de plaques,
Sous le bronze, la soie et les brillantes laques,
Semble un crustacé noir, gigantesque et vermeil.

Il l'a vue. Il sourit dans la barbe du masque,
Et son pas plus hâtif fait reluire au soleil
Les deux antennes d'or qui tremblent à son casque.

The sequence of *Les Trophées* closes with a series of selected sonnets entitled "Nature and Dream." In these the poet quits the field of history, and concentrates his vision on such episodes of modern life and landscape as are specially sympathetic to him. He admits many things here that help us to form an exact impression of his own mind. He dwells with affectionate complacency over the destruction of all that made Sicily what she was in antiquity, and the durability amid the general wreck of a few coins in which the beauty of the Sicilian virgins is still immortal. He raises a picture of the gorgeous funerals of ancient Greek warriors, descending to Hades surrounded by all the pomp and glory of their fellow-countrymen, while the French poet himself will one of these days share the inglorious burial which is administered in turn to all members of the democracy :

> *Et pourtant j'ai rêvé ce destin glorieux*
> *De tomber au soleil ainsi que les aïeux,*
> *Jeune encore et pleuré des héros et des vierges.*

In his aspect of nature, in his moods towards life as it manifests itself to us to-day, there is no petulance but a marked and ever-present sense of regretful loss, only to be redeemed by a passionate and vivid realisation of scenes and objects otherwise lost for ever.

It should, perhaps, be added here that the volume of *Les Trophées* is not entirely devoted to sonnets. There are three mediæval Spanish romances, composed in *terza rima*, and a somewhat extended epical study, in couplets, called *Les Conquerants de l'Or*. Each of these is vigorously written, and worthy of study, but neither induces the critical reader to waver in his conviction that the sonnet was the province of poetry which M. de Heredia was born to occupy.

Nor has he confined himself entirely to verse. M. de Heredia is the author of a translation, in four large volumes, of *La Conquête du Mexique* of Bernal Diaz, in which, by a sustained effort of style, he has transformed the entire narrative into such French of the sixteenth century as Agrippa d'Aubigné might have signed. Lastly, in 1894, in a little book illustrated by Daniel Vierge, the poet gave us a version of that curious picaresque romance, *La Nonne Alferez*.

III

To call José-Maria de Heredia a great poet would be to misuse language. He lacks the breadth and humanity of the leaders of poetry. But, beyond all question, he is a great poetic artist and probably the most remarkable now alive in Europe. The few quotations which I have been able to give in the preceding pages will undoubtedly be enough to prove this fact to any who have not yet made the acquaintance of his work; and M. de Heredia is none of those writers from whom an indulgent reviewer can select pieces which give an impression of far higher merit than the perusal of the actual volume justifies.

Perhaps his most singular characteristic, the evidence of a self-control almost without parallel in recent literature, is the high level of workmanship which runs through his entire published poetry. He must sometimes write poor verse, one fancies, since he is mortal, but at least he never publishes it. Some numbers in *Les Trophées* are more interesting than others; it is difficult to admit that any are better written. From beginning to end the book rings with melody, each sonnet brings up before the inward eye a luminous picture, in a clear sunlit atmosphere, flashing with colour, sharply defined, completely provided with every artifice and accomplishment of learning, taste, and craftsmanship. The only objection, indeed, which one is inclined to bring against M. de Heredia as a poet is the result of this uniform strenuousness. One wishes that all were not quite so metallic in sound, so sumptuous in colour, so radiantly and sonorously objective. The softer stop is missed, the pathetic and mysterious qualities are neglected. But in these slipshod days, it is no small thing to find that poets still exist who hold their art in chivalric honour, and who would rather be banished from their country than allow a loose rhyme to escape them, or commit a solecism in prosody.

1894.

WALTER PATER

Walter Pater

A PORTRAIT

FEW recent events can have surprised and saddened the sincere lovers of literature more than the death, in middle life, of Walter Pater. A peculiar vexation, so to speak, was added to the natural grief such a loss must have caused, by the strange inexactitude, in matters of detail, which marked almost all the notices of his career which appeared at the time. In most of these notices, it is true, there was manifested a wish to pay homage to one of the most exquisite, the most self-respecting, the most individual prose-writers of the age; but knowledge, especially of his earlier years and intellectual development, was lacking. He was one who never had tempted the interviewer, who had never chatted to the press about himself, and facts regarding him were not at that abrupt moment forthcoming.

How far accidents of time and place were responsible for aiding this condition of things it were now perhaps idle to speculate. The fame of Walter Pater will not be wrecked on the holiday of an editor or the indolence of a reporter. It is grounded on the respect which has not yet failed to follow pure and distinguished excellence in the art of writing. As years go on, he will more and more find his admirers, the rescuers of his renown. A subtle and penetrating essay by Mr. Lionel Johnson (in the *Fortnightly Review* for September 1894) has already pointed the way to those whose business it will be to detect Pater's influence upon his age, and to illustrate the individual merits of his style. In the following pages an attempt will be made to present the facts of the uneventful career of the author of *Marius*, so oddly travestied at the moment of his death, with some regard to continuity and truth. In preparing this sketch, I have had the encouragement and the help of the surviving members of his family, without whose co-operation I should not have undertaken such a task.

I

A very considerable interest attaches to the parentage of Walter Pater. His family was of Dutch extraction, his immediate ancestors having, it is believed, come over from the Low Countries with William of Orange. It was said, and our friend loved to believe it, that the court-painter, Jean Baptiste Pater, the pupil of Watteau, was of the same stock. If so, the relationship must have been collateral and not direct, for when the creator of so many delicate *fêtes champêtres* was painting in Flanders—he died in 1736—the English Paters had already settled at Olney, in Buckinghamshire, where they lived all through the eighteenth century. Reserved and shy, preserving many of their Dutch customs, they are described in family tradition as mixing little with their neighbours, and as keeping through several generations this curious custom, that, while the sons were always brought up as Roman Catholics, the daughters were no less invariably trained in the Anglican faith. The father of Walter Pater quitted the Roman Church before his marriage, without adopting any other form of faith, and his two sons were the first Paters who were not brought up as Catholics.

Towards the close of the eighteenth century, the poet Cowper was the fellow-townsman and the friend of the Dutch emigrants in Olney, and the family long possessed some of his verses in his own manuscript. The son of the man who had known Cowper quitted the Buckinghamshire household, and went out to America. He settled in New York, associating chiefly with the Dutch colony in that city; here his son, Richard Glode Pater, the father of the critic, was born. The family came back in the beginning of the present century, and settled at Shadwell, on the north shore of the Thames, between Wapping and Stepney, a situation now of extreme squalor, but eighty years ago still considered countrified and pleasant. Here, after his father's death, Richard Glode Pater continued to live, a medical practitioner working, mainly for the love of them, among poor folks in the East End, refusing to move into a more fashionable quarter, and despoiling himself of his patrimony by his constant benevolence.

To the house in Shadwell, Richard Glode Pater brought Maria Hill as his wife, and here were born to him four children, two of them sons, of whom Walter was the second. The elder son, William Thomson Pater, adopted his father's profession, and became the head of a large lunatic asylum. He died unmarried, on April 24, 1887, at the age of fifty-two, "quitting," in his brother's words, "a useful and happy life." In him, however, with the exception of a marked pleasure in being surrounded with pretty objects, not a single feature had ever shown itself of the peculiar intellectual characteristics or tastes of his brother. The future critic was born at Shadwell, on August 4, 1839, receiving the names Walter Horatio, in compliment to a cousin who survives him.

Richard Glode Pater died so early that his second son scarcely remembered him in later life. The mother and grandmother left the house in Shadwell, and went to live with a sister of the former at Enfield, where the children were brought up. In the retired neighbourhood of Chase Side they took a house, which has since been pulled down; it possessed a large, old-fashioned garden, in which the children found great delight. It would be an error to trace in the imaginary portrait, called *The Child in the House*, a definite picture of the early surroundings of Walter Pater. The existence at Enfield is hardly touched upon there, with the sole exception of the "cry on the stair," announcing the death of Florian Deleal's father; this, it appears, is a reminiscence of the decease, not of his father, but of his grandmother, which was so announced to the household at Enfield. So far as *The Child in the House* depicts a veritable scene, it presents to us Fish Hall, near Hadlow, Kent, the residence of his godmother and cousin, Mrs. Walter H. May; this mansion, part of which was very old, was the favourite holiday-haunt of the little Paters, and a place of mystery and romance to Walter.

If, however, *The Child in the House* must be accepted very guardedly as giving an impression of the physical surroundings of Walter Pater's childhood, much more of actual reminiscence has been put into *Emerald Uthwart* (a story now reprinted in the *Miscellaneous Studies*). The first elements of education were given at the private house of the head-master of the grammar-school at Enfield, but the earliest crisis of Pater's life was the entrance into King's School, Canterbury, at the age of fourteen. The "old ecclesiastical city," to which Emerald proceeds, is Canterbury, closely and exactly described, and the features enumerated in the story— "the curiosities of the Precincts, the 'dark entry,' the rich heraldries of the blackened and mouldering cloister, the ruined overgrown spaces where the old monastery stood, the stones of which furnished material for the rambling prebends' houses"—these were features at Canterbury which immediately impressed the imagination of the shy and sensitive little boy, and remained with him through life as having given him his earliest experience of æsthetic pleasure.

It seems probable that, on the whole, this part of *Emerald Uthwart* may be taken as strictly autobiographical. Pater was happy at King's School, in spite of his complete indifference to outdoor games. In his first years at public school he was very idle and backward, nor was it till he reached the sixth form that his faculties seemed really to awaken. He is remembered as rather a popular boy, and as years went on his unquestioned ability inspired respect On the day of Pater's funeral the Warden of Keble preached in the Cathedral of Canterbury, and was able to record, in touching phrases, the pride which the school had always felt in him, and Pater's own persistent attachment to the school. From the first, and before he went to Canterbury, Walter had been considered the "clever" one of the family; not specially precocious, he was always meditative and serious—marked from the very first for the intellectual life. It is interesting to note that, quite without prompting from without, and while still at Enfield, all his thoughts were turned towards the Church. He loved best to organise a sort of solemn processional game, in which he took the part of bishop or cardinal. From the time when he first began to think of a future condition, his design was to be a clergyman; never, curiously enough, a priest in the religion of his fathers, but in the Anglican ritual. Throughout life, it may here be said, even in his later days, when his thoughts turned back more and more to theological pre-occupations, Walter Pater never had any serious leaning towards Rome. Yet there can be little question that the heritage of his ancestors, in their obstinate adhesion to Catholicism, had much to do with his haunting sense of the value of the sensuous emblem, the pomp of colour and melody, in the offices of religion. These tendencies had received a great impetus while he was yet a little boy, and had not proceeded to Canterbury, from a visit he paid to a young friend who lived at Hursley. Here he attracted the attention of Keble, who walked and talked much with him, and encouraged him in his religious aspirations. Pater retained through life a vivid recollection of this saintly man, although he never saw him again.

Shortly before he left school, as he was entering his twentieth year, Pater read *Modern Painters*, and came very abruptly under the influence of Ruskin. The world of art was now for the first time opened to him. It is necessary at this point to refute an extraordinary fable, widely circulated at the time of his death, to the effect that the finished and beautiful essay on "Winckelmann" was written, and even printed, while the author was a schoolboy at Canterbury. The idea is preposterous; it was not until many years later that Pater became aware of the existence of the German critic, and his essay was composed and published long after he was a Fellow of Brasenose. It is singular, indeed, that he is not known to have made any attempt to write, either as a schoolboy or an undergraduate, his earliest essays being as mature in style as the author was mature in years. Pater made no painful experiments in authorship, or, if he did, he kept them to himself. He did not begin to practise the art of writing until he had mastered all its secrets.

On June 11, 1858, he entered Queen's College, Oxford, as a commoner, with an exhibition from Canterbury; and four years later, in the Michaelmas Term of 1862, he took his degree, gaining only a second class in *Literæ Humaniores*. Of these years of his undergraduate life it does not appear that there is much to reveal. In bare rooms, in the dim back quadrangle of his College, Pater worked quietly and unobtrusively, making few friends, very shy and silent, hardly observed in the noisy Oxford life of thirty-five years ago. He was the pupil of Mr. W. W. Capes, now rector of Liphook, then bursar and tutor of Queen's, and amongst those very rare spirits who divined the man he was to be was his earliest friend, Mr. Ingram Bywater, now Regius Professor of Greek. It is not understood that during these undergraduate days Pater's mind, a seed slowly germinating in the darkness, showed much partiality for pure literature or for plastic art. He was fascinated mainly by the study of logic and metaphysic, which were his pastimes, while the laborious business of classical scholarship occupied all but his leisure moments. Whether any record of these silent years remains, even with the few friends who shared them, seems doubtful. Pater never kept a diary, rarely wrote letters, and at this time offered no salient points for observation to seize upon. Yet one far-seeing man had noted the peculiar originality of Pater's temperament. Having in the ordinary course of his studies submitted some work to Jowett, that astute observer was so much struck with his power that he very generously offered to coach him for nothing. The offer was gratefully accepted, and Pater used to describe the thrill of gratification, and, still more, of astonishment, which he experienced when Jowett said to him one day, as he was taking his leave: "I think you have a mind that will come to great eminence." Unhappily, some years after there was a complete estrangement of sympathy between Jowett and Pater. But it is pleasant to record that, in the last year of the life of each, it was removed, and that Jowett was among those who congratulated Pater most cordially on his *Plato and Platonism*.

In 1862—his degree had been a disappointment—Pater, now three-and-twenty, took rooms in the High Street, Oxford, and read with private pupils. Of these Mr. T. H. S. Escott has told us in his pleasant reminiscences of Oxford that he was one. Another pupil, of somewhat later date, was Mr. Charles Lancelot Shadwell, now Fellow of Oriel, destined to become the most intimate of all Pater's friends, and now the guardian and editor of his papers. But still no definite aim seemed to have revealed itself to the future critic; he was reading and meditating deeply, but he had as yet no call to create. Time went by; in 1864 Pater was elected a Fellow of Brasenose College, and went into residence there. With this change in his material existence, a change came over his mind. His sympathies grew wider and more human, he became more of a student of poetry, he formed more friendships, and was more assiduous in their cultivation. Of his earliest efforts after literary expression, all, it is believed, were destroyed by himself, with the solitary exception of the little study of a pure and brilliant spirit of youth, called "Diaphaneitè," of which the MS., dated July 1864, was found after his death and published by Mr. Shadwell in the *Miscellaneous Studies* of 1895. At last, in 1866, at the age of twenty-seven, he ventured to write and to print a little essay, a note or fragment, on Coleridge. We may read this first expression of a new writer to-day in the *Appreciations*. We shall find little of the peculiar charm of the mature Pater. His interest is solely in Coleridge, the metaphysician, the critic of thought; that this same philosopher was an exquisite poet has not occurred to him, he positively forgets to mention the fact. As far as style is concerned, the little essay is correct and cold, without oddity, but with little trace of the harmonious felicity which was about to develop.

Vast is the change when we meet Walter Pater next. He had come from school with a tendency to value all things German. The teaching of Jowett and of T. H. Green tended to strengthen this habit, but Mr. Capes warned him against its excess, and endeavoured, at first with but little success, to attract him to the lucidity and gaiety of French literature. Pater's studies in philosophy now naturally brought him to Goethe, so massive an influence in the Oxford of that day, and the teaching of Goethe laid a deep impress upon his temperament, upon his whole outlook on the intellectual life. It was natural that one so delicately sensitive to the external symbol as was Pater should be prepared by the companionship of Goethe for the influence of a man who was

Goethe's master in this one direction, and it was to a spirit inflammable in the highest degree that in 1866 was laid the torch of Otto Jahn's Life of Winckelmann, the *Biographische Aufsätze*. There was everything in the character and career of the great German restorer of Hellenic feeling to fascinate Pater, who seemed, through Ruskin, Goethe and Hegel, to have travelled to his true prototype, to the one personality among the dead which was completely in sympathy with his own. Pater, too, among the sandhills of a spiritual Brandenburg, had held out arms of longing towards ideal beauty, revealed in physical or sensuous forms, yet inspired and interpenetrated with harmonious thought. The troubled feverish vision, the variegated and indeed over-decorated æsthetic of Ruskin, had become wearisome to Pater—not simple enough nor sensuous enough. Winckelmann was the master he wanted, who could "finger those pagan marbles with unsinged hands, with no sense of shame or loss," who could live serenely "in a world of exquisite but abstract and colourless form;" and it was with the study of Winckelmann that he became himself a writer.

His famous essay on "Winckelmann" was the result of this new enthusiasm. It was published in the *Westminster Review* for January 1867, the author being now in his twenty-eighth year. From this time Pater's advance, though slow, was unbroken. Mr. John Morley having, in 1867, taken the editorship of the *Fortnightly Review*, called around him immediately a group of the most brilliant young men of the day. Walter Pater was in no undue haste to respond to the appeal. In 1868, inventing a name which has since sunken into disrepute and even ridicule, he wrote an essay on "Æsthetic Poetry," in which the early work of Mr. William Morris received prompt and judicious analysis. Then followed the series which are still so potent in their peculiar charm, the magnificent and most characteristic "Notes on Lionardo de Vinci," in November 1869; the "Fragment on Sandro Botticelli" in August 1870; the "Pico della Mirandula" in October, and the "Michelangelo" in November 1871. In 1873 most of these, and others, were published together in the memorable volume originally entitled *Studies in the History of the Renaissance.*

At this point he became partly famous. We may look back over the years which followed his fellowship, and see that, with the accession of humanistic ideas, he had gradually lost all belief in the Christian religion. This was the point, in his whole career, at which he was furthest from the Anglican faith. His intention, on relinquishing the idea of entering the Church of England, had been to become a Unitarian minister. This also he had abandoned by 1864. But that Pater's interest in ecclesiastical matters was never really dead, and that it soon began to revive, is proved by an anecdote with which the Bishop of Peterborough obliges me. He remembers dining with him in 1873, in company with Bonamy Price. Conversation turned on ecclesiastical matters, and Pater passed on to a dreamy monologue about the beauty of the Reserved

Sacrament in Roman churches, which "gave them all the sentiment of a house where lay a dead friend." This immediately aroused the Protestantism of Bonamy Price, and a theological discussion ensued which waxed so warm that Dr. Creighton had to suggest a retreat to the drawing-room. When he came up for election at Brasenose it was as a non-clerical fellow—I think the first who ever was appointed there—that Pater took his place in the society. In the next year, in company with Mr. Shadwell, he paid his first visit to Italy, and at Ravenna, Pisa, Florence, formed those impressions of the art of the Renaissance which were so powerfully to colour all his own future work as an artist. In 1858, when he came to Oxford, his sisters had migrated to Heidelberg, and here it was his custom to spend the long vacation, making no friends among the Germans, however, and never, in all those years, troubling himself to learn to speak their language.

II

The costume of Walter Pater had been the ordinary academic dress of the don of the period, but in May 1869 he flashed forth at the Private View of the Royal Academy in a new top hat and a silk tie of brilliant apple-green. This little transformation marked a crisis; he was henceforth no longer a provincial philosopher, but a critic linked to London and the modern arts. Where he touched the latter was through the Preraphaelites, especially through the extreme admiration he had conceived for the works of Mr. Burne-Jones, then much talked about, but rarely seen. At no time, I think, had he much personal knowledge either of that painter or of Rossetti. With Mr. Swinburne he became about that date more intimate. The poet was a not unfrequent visitor in those years to Pater's college rooms. To all young Oxford, then, the name of Mr. Swinburne was an enchantment, and there used to be envious traditions of an upper window in Brasenose Lane thrown open to the summer night, and, welling forth from it, a music of verse which first outsang and then silenced the nightingales, protracting its harmonies until it disconcerted the lark himself at sunrise.

After this, it is a notable instance of the art of sinking to record that I first set eyes on Pater in 1871, as he and Mr. Swinburne were dismounting from a hansom cab at Gabriel Rossetti's door in Cheyne Walk. Almost unknown to the world, he was already an object of respect to me as the author of those "Notes on Lionardo," which had seemed to give a new aspect to the whole conception of Italian art. In 1872 I was presented to him in the studio of William Bell Scott: it was not until the early months of 1874 that I first began to visit him at Oxford, and so opened a friendship which was never clouded for a moment in the course of more than twenty years. From this point, then, although my opportunities of seeing Pater, especially in Oxford, were but occasional, I can record something from personal knowledge.

In 1869, removing from Brasenose many of the

pretty objects and *bric-à-brac* with which he had been the first man in Oxford to decorate college rooms, Pater furnished a little house in Norham Gardens, No. 2 Bradmore Road, his sisters returning from Heidelberg to keep house for him. Once settled here, Pater blossomed out into considerable sociability, entertaining and being entertained in the cordial Oxford way. He had now a large circle of pleasant acquaintances; I cannot remember that he had many intimate friends. Besides those whom I have mentioned already, I can but recall Mark Pattison, Dr. Mandell Creighton (now Bishop of Peterborough), and Miss Mary Arnold, soon to marry an accomplished young member of Pater's own college, Mr. Humphry Ward. To these he would doubtless talk, to each in a different way, of the interests most deeply rooted in his heart, "of charm, and lucid order, and labour of the file," and to a very few London friends also. The rest of the world found him affable and acquiescent, already in those remote days displaying a little of that Renan manner which later on became emphasised, a manner which trifled gracefully and somewhat mysteriously with a companion not entirely in sympathy.

Pater's relation to the Rector of Lincoln was amusing. It was at once confiding and suspicious. "Pattison is charming," he used to murmur, "when he's good. Shall we go over and see if he is good this afternoon?" But he was worried by a certain wilfulness in the Rector; he could prove to be so far from good, so absolutely naughty. I remember on one occasion—I think in the autumn of 1875—when the Rector, on a visit at Bradmore Road, had been delicious: he had talked, in his most distinguished way, on a dozen rare and exquisite topics. He left, begging Pater to come to him next day, and kindly extending the invitation to me. Accordingly we went, but the charm was broken. A frivolous demon had entered into the Rector; he talked of croquet and of petticoats. We went back, sad and silent, to Bradmore Road, and, just as we reached home, Pater said, with solemn firmness, "What Pattison likes best in the world, no doubt, is romping with great girls in the gooseberry-bushes!"

The vacations in these years were very pleasant to Pater; they were almost always spent abroad—in France, in the company of his sisters. He would walk as much as possible, scouring a neighbourhood for architectural features, and preserving those impressions of travel, which most of us lament to find so fugitive, with astonishing exactitude. He was no linguist, and French was the only language in which he could even make his wants understood. Although so much in Germany in his youth, he could speak no German. When he was travelling he always left a place, if any one staying in the hotel spoke to him. He had no wish to be competent in modern languages; he used to say: "Between you and me and the post, I hate a foreigner," and when exotic persons of distinction threatened to visit Brasenose, Pater used to disappear until he was sure that they had gone. He loved the North of

France extremely, and knew it well. He was always planning a series of studies on the great ecclesiastical towns of France, yet wrote no more than a couple of these—on Amiens and on Vézelay. So eagerly did he prosecute these holiday tours, that he habitually over-walked himself, thus losing much of the benefit which he might otherwise have gained from the only form of exercise he ever indulged in. I note, in a letter of 1877, describing a visit to Azay-le-Rideau, this characteristic sentence: "We find always great pleasure in adding to our experiences of these French places, and return always a little tired indeed, but with our minds pleasantly full of memories of stained glass, old tapestries, and new wild flowers." These excursions rarely extended further than the centre of France, but once, I think in 1882, Pater went alone to Rome, and spent the winter vacation there. He could ill endure exciting travel, or too rapid hurrying from one impressive place to another. His eye absorbed so slowly, and his memory retained what he saw so completely, that to be shown too much was almost physical pain to him, and yet he was always inflicting it upon himself.

Some time after I knew him first, that entertaining skit, *The New Republic*, was produced, and achieved great popular success. Pater had his niche in this gallery of caricatures, under the title of Mr. Rose. It has been represented that he suffered violent distress from this parody of his style and manner, that it caused him to retire from society and to abandon the prosecution of literature. Nothing in the world could be further from the truth. He thought the portrait a little unscrupulous, and he was discomposed by the freedom of some of its details. But he admired the cleverness and promise of the book, and it did not cause him to alter his mode of life or thought in the smallest degree. He was even flattered, for he was an author much younger and more obscure than most of those who were satirised, and he was sensible that to be thus distinguished was a compliment. What he liked less, what did really ruffle him, was the persistence with which the newspapers at this time began to attribute to him all sorts of "æsthetic" follies and extravagances. He said to me, in 1876: "I wish they wouldn't call me 'a hedonist'; it produces such a bad effect on the minds of people who don't know Greek." And the direct result of all these journalistic mosquito-bites was the suppression of the famous "Conclusion" in the second (1877) edition of his *Renaissance*.

The source of his very long silence—for twelve years divided his second book from his first—I hardly know, unless it be attributed to the painful slowness of his methods of composition, and his extreme solicitude for perfection of style. At last, in February, 1885, was published his romance of *Marius the Epicurean*, the work by which, I believe, Pater will pre-eminently be known to posterity. In the meantime had appeared, in the *Fortnightly Review* for 1876, several of those Greek studies, on Demeter and Persephone, on the Marbles of Ægina and the like, which Mr. Shadwell collected in a posthumous volume in 1895; *The Child in the*

House, too, in its earliest form, belongs to 1878, though first published as a book in the summer of 1894. The success of *Marius* was as great as that of a book so grave and strenuous could be. In 1887 Pater followed it by a series of four *Imaginary Portraits*, studies in philosophic fiction, one of which, "Denys l'Auxerrois," displays the peculiarities of his style with more concentrated splendour than any other of his writings. In 1889 he collected some of his miscellaneous critical studies into a volume called *Appreciations, with an Essay on Style*. In 1893 he published his highly finished college lectures on *Plato and Platonism* in a volume of rare dignity and humanistic beauty. Finally, in the early summer of 1894, *The Child in the House* was issued from the Oxford Press of Mr. Daniel, as a precious toy for bibliomaniacs. This list of publications practically resumes the events in Pater's life through twenty years.

During that period the household was moved once, in 1886, to Kensington, and again, in 1893, back to Oxford, where he fitted up a house in St. Giles. But, all the while, Pater's real home was in his rooms at Brasenose, where he passed a quiet, cloistered, and laborious existence, divided between his college duties and his books. His later years were comforted by a great deal of consideration and affection from those around him; noiseless, as he was, and in a sense unexhilarating, he became increasingly an object of respectful admiration to young Oxford men, whom, on his part, he treated with the most courteous indulgence.

Of this generation, one disciple came to proffer a tribute of hero-worship, and remained to become an intimate friend; this was the Rev. F. W. Bussell, now Fellow of Brasenose, whose tender solicitude did much to render the latest of Pater's years agreeable to him. Pater acted for some time as dean and tutor of his college, entering assiduously into the councils and discipline of the society, but he never accepted, if indeed it were ever offered, any university office. He shrank from all multiplication of responsibility, from anything which should break in upon the sequestered and austere simplicity of his life. As time went on, a great change came over his relation to religious matters. When I had known him first he was a pagan, without any guide but that of the personal conscience; years brought gradually with them a greater and greater longing for the supporting solace of a creed. His talk, his habits, became more and more theological, and it is my private conviction that, had he lived a few years longer, he would have endeavoured to take orders and a small college living in the country.

Report, which found so much to misrepresent in a life so orderly and simple, has erred even as to the place and occasion of his death. He was taken ill with rheumatic fever in the month of June 1894, being, as he remained to the end, not in college, but with his sisters in their house in St. Giles. He was recovering, and was well enough to be busy upon a study on *Pascal*, which he has left nearly completed, when, in consequence of writing too close to an open window, pleurisy set in and greatly reduced his strength. Again he seemed convalescent, and had left his room, without ill-effect, on July 29, when, repeating the experiment next day, the action of the heart failed, and he died, on the staircase of his house, in the arms of his sister, at ten o'clock on the morning of Monday, July 30, 1894. Had he lived five days longer, he would have completed his fifty-fifth year. He was buried, in the presence of many of his oldest friends, in the beautiful cemetery of St. Giles at Oxford.

III

When Pater was first seized with an ambition to write, the individuals of his own age with whom he came into competition were mainly poets. Those were the early days of Gabriel and Christina Rossetti, of Morris, of Swinburne; and most of the still younger men made their first steps in the field of verse, however far they might afterwards diverge from it. Pater, in this nest of singing-birds, resolved to be in prose no less painstaking, no less elaborate, no less bound by rule and art than the poets were. He is to be distinguished from those who had so much to say that their speech was forced out of them in a torrent, nor less from those whose instinct led them to bubble forth in periods of a natural artless grace. If we take these symbols of a mountain-stream or of a fountain for other prose-writers who have won the ear of the public with little effort, then for Pater the appropriate image seems the artesian well, to reach the contents of of which, strata of impermeable clay must be laboriously bored. It was not that there was any lack of material there, nor any doubt about the form it must take when it emerged, but that it was so miraculously deep down and hard to reach. I have known writers of every degree, but never one to whom the act of composition was such a travail and an agony as it was to Pater.

In his earlier years the labour of lifting the sentences was so terrific that any one with less fortitude would have entirely abandoned the effort. I recollect the writing of the opening chapters of *Marius*, and the stress that attended it—the intolerable languor and fatigue, the fevers and the cold fits, the grey hours of lassitude and insomnia, the toil as at a deep petroleum well when the oil refuses to flow. With practice, this terrific effort grew less. A year or two ago I was reminding him of those old times of storm and stress, and he replied, "Ah! it is much easier now. If I live long enough, no doubt I shall learn quite to like writing." The public saw the result of the labour in the smooth solidity of the result, and could suppose, from the very elaboration, that great pains had been taken. How much pains, very few indeed can have guessed!

It may be of interest to record the manner in which this most self-conscious and artistic of prose-writers proceeded. First of all, another pretty fable must be knocked on the head. It has been said, and repeated, that Pater composed his best sentences without any relation to a context, and wrote them down on little squares of paper, ready to stick them in at appropriate and effective places. This is nonsense; it is quite true that he used such squares of paper, but it was for a very different purpose. He read with a box of these squares beside him, jotting down on each, very roughly, anything in his author which struck his fancy, either giving an entire quotation, or indicating a reference, or noting a disposition. He did not begin, I think, any serious critical work without surrounding himself by dozens of these little loose notes. When they were not direct references or citations, they were of the nature of a *memoria technica*. Here is an example:

"Something about the gloomy Byzantine archit., belfries, solemn night come in about the birds attracted by the Towers."

Here is another:

"? did he suppose predestination to have taken place, only *after* the Fall?"

These papers would be placed about him, like the pieces of a puzzle, and when the right moment came the proper square would serve as a monitor or as a guide.

Having prepared his box of little squares, he would begin the labour of actual composition, and so conscious was he of the modifications and additions which would supervene that he always wrote on ruled paper, leaving each alternate line blank. Mr. Austin Dobson reminds me that Goldsmith did the same. On this broad canvas of alternate lines, then, Pater would slowly begin to draw his composition, the cartoon of

what would in time be a finished essay. In the first
draft the phrase would be a bald one; in the blank
alternate line he would at leisure insert fresh descriptive
or parenthetical clauses, other adjectives, more exquisitely related adverbs, until the space was filled.
It might then be supposed that the MS. was complete.
Far from it! Cancelling sheet by sheet, Pater then
began to copy out the whole—as before, on alternate
lines of copy-book pages; this revise was treated in
the same way—corrected, enlarged, interleaved, as it
were, with minuter shades of feeling and more elaborate
apparatus of parenthesis.

No wonder that certain disadvantages were attendant
upon the excessive finish of such a style. It is not
possible to work in this way, with a cold hammer, and
yet to avoid a certain deadness and slipperiness of
surface. Pater's periods, in attaining their long-drawn
harmony and fulness, were apt to lose vigour. Their
polish did not quite make up for their languor, for the
faintness and softness which attended their slow
manipulation. Verse will bear an almost endless labour
of the file; prose, as the freer and more spontaneous
form, is less happy in subjection to it. "What long
sentences Plato writes!" Pater says in his *Platonism*,
and no doubt Plato might return the compliment.
The sentences of the Oxford critic are often too long,
and they are sometimes broken-backed with havimg
had to bear too heavy a burden of allusion and illustration. His style, however, was his peculiarity. It
had beautiful qualities, if we have to confess that it

had the faults of those qualities. It was highly individual; it cannot be said that he owed it to any other writer, or that at any period of his thirty years of literary labour he faltered or swerved from his own path. He was to a high degree self-centred. Pater did not study his contemporaries; a year or two ago, he told me that he had read scarcely a chapter of Mr. Stevenson and not a line of Mr. Kipling. "I feel, from what I hear about them," he said, "that they are strong; they might lead me out of my path. I want to go on writing in my own way, good or bad. I should be afraid to read Kipling, lest he should come between me and my page next time I sat down to write." It was the excess of a very native and genuine modesty. He, too, was strong, had he but known it, strong enough to have resisted the magnets of contemporary style. Perhaps his own writing might have grown a little simpler and a little more supple if he had had the fortitude to come down and fight among his fellows.

IV

Walter Pater was another of those discreet spirits who, like Gray, "never speak out." He was cautious, reserved, and shy in his relations even with his friends; he seemed to possess no medium through which to approach them very closely. An extremely affectionate disposition took the place of expansiveness, and the young people who in later years gathered around him mistook the one for the other. Each found in Pater what he brought; each saw in that patient, courteous, indulgent mirror a pleasant reflection of himself. The inaccessibility of Pater is another of those fables which have to be destroyed; no one was less a hermit, no one was more easily amused or better pleased to bid a congenial companion welcome. He was an assiduous host, a gracious listener; but who could tell what was passing behind those half-shut, dark-grey eyes, that courteous and gentle mask? He liked the human race, one is inclined to say, liked its noise and neighbourhood, if it were neither too loud nor too near, but his faith in it was never positive, nor would he trust it to read his secret thoughts.

I have already suggested his likeness to Renan in the attitude of his mind. The great Frenchman has described, in his autobiography, the tendency which led him to refrain from opposition and argument, and to bow the head in the conversational house of Rimmon. Walter Pater had these concessions, mere escapes of the soul from undue pressure, and he had, too, quite unconsciously, some of the very tricks of speech of Renan—especially the "no doubt" that answered to the Frenchman's incessant "n'en doutez pas." With natures like his, in which the tide of physical spirits runs low, in which the vitality is lukewarm, the first idea in the presence of anything too vivacious is retreat, and the most obvious form of social retreat is what we call "affectation." It is not to be denied that, in the old days, Pater, startled by strangers, was apt to seem affected: he retreated as into a fortress, and enclosed himself in a sort of solemn effeminacy. It was, at its worst, mild in comparison with what the masters of preposterous behaviour have since accustomed us to, but it reminded one too much of Mr. Rose. It was put on entirely for the benefit of strangers, and to his inner circle of friends it seemed like a joke. Perhaps in some measure it was a joke; no one could ever quite tell whether Pater's strange *rictus* was closer to laughter or to tears.

A nature so enclosed as his, so little capable of opening its doors to others, must have some outlet of relief. Pater found his outlet in a sort of delicate, secret playfulness. There are animals which sit all day immovable and humped up among the riot of their fellows, and which, when all the rest of the menagerie is asleep, steal out upon their slip of greensward and play the wildest pranks in the light of the moon. Pater has often reminded me of some such armadillo or wombat. That childishness which is the sign-manual of genius used to come out in the oddest way when he was perfectly at home. Those who think of him as a solemn pundit of æsthetics may be amazed to know that he delighted in very simple and farcical spectacles and in the broadest of humour. His favourite among modern playwrights was Mr. Pinero, and I shall never forget going with him to see *The Magistrate*, when that piece was originally produced. Not a schoolboy in the house was more convulsed with laughter, more enchanted at the romping "business" of the play, than the author of *Marius*. He had the gift, when I knew him first, of inventing little farcical dialogues, into which he introduced his contemporaries; in these the Rector of Lincoln generally figured, and Pater had a rare art of imitating Pattison's speech and peevish intonation. One playful fancy, persisted in so long that even close and old friends were deceived by it, was the figment of a group of relations—Uncle Capsicum and Uncle Guava, Aunt Fancy (who fainted when the word "leg" was mentioned), and Aunt Tart (for whom no acceptable present could ever be found). These shadowy personages had been talked about for so many years that at last, I verily believe, Pater had almost persuaded himself of their existence. Perhaps these little touches will be thought too trifling to be mentioned, but I hold that they were all a part and parcel of his complex and shrouded intellectual life, and therefore not to be forgotten.

He had great sweetness and uniformity of temper, and almost the only thing that ever ruffled him was a reference to an act of vandalism committed at Brasenose while he was on the governing body. The college had a group, called "Cain and Abel," cast in lead, a genuine work by John of Bologna. For some reason or other this was thought inconvenient, and was sold for old lead, a somewhat barbarous proceeding. Pater, from indolence, or else from indifference to late Italian sculpture, did not stir a finger to prevent this desecration, and in later years a perfectly unfailing mode of rousing him would be to say, artlessly, "Was there not once a group by John of Bologna in the college?" However sunken in reverie, however dreamily detached, Pater would sit up in a moment, and say, with great acidity, "It was totally devoid of merit, no doubt."

Pater showed much tact and good sense in his attitude towards the college life. He lectured rarely, I believe, in later years; in the old days he was an assiduous tutor. His temperament, it is true, sometimes made it difficult to work with him. On one occasion, at the examination for scholarships, he undertook to look over the English essays; when the examiners met to compare marks, Pater had none. He explained, with languor, "They did not much impress me." As something had to be done, he was asked to endeavour to recall such impressions as he had formed; to stimulate his memory, the names were read out in alphabetical order. Pater shook his head mournfully as each was pronounced, murmuring dreamily, "I do not recall him," "He did not strike me," and so on. At last the reader came to the name of Sanctuary, on which Pater's face lit up, and he said, "Yes; I remember; I liked his name."

My friend, Dr. Henry Jackson, gives me an anecdote which illustrates a more practical side to his character. In 1870, having just begun to lecture at Trinity, our Cambridge Platonist found himself seated next Pater at dinner in Brasenose. He said to him: "I believe you lecture constantly on *The Republic*. How do you get through it in time? It seems as though lecturing three times a week for three terms, it would be impossible to deal adequately within a year with all the problems and the fallacies." "Oh!" said Pater, "I always begin by telling them that Socrates is not such a fool as he seems, and we get through nicely in two terms." He grew more and more inclined to take an indulgent view of the young people. A year or two ago, I remember his saying, when somebody asked him whether the horse-play of the undergraduates did not disturb him, "Oh! no; I rather enjoy it. They are like playful young tigers, that have been fed." He was not a "progressive"; our friend the Bishop of Peterborough recalls a serious discussion in common-room at Brasenose, on the burning subject of university reform. Pater interposed in the thick of the fray with the somewhat disconcerting remark, "I do not know what your object is. At present the undergraduate is a child of nature; he grows up like a wild rose in a country lane; you want to turn him into a turnip, rob him of all grace, and plant him out in rows." And his remark, concerning bonfires in the quad, that they lighted up the spire of St. Mary's so beautifully, will long be remembered.

The perennial conflict in his members, between his exquisite instinct for corporeal beauty on the one hand and his tendency to ecclesiastical symbol and theological dogma on the other, is the secret, I think, of what made the character of Pater so difficult for others to elucidate, in some measure also so painful and confusing for himself. He was not all for Apollo, nor all for Christ, but each deity swayed in him, and neither had that perfect homage that brings peace behind it. As Alphonse Daudet says of some thinker, " Son cerveau était une cathédrale désaffectée," and when he tried, as he bade us try, "to burn always with the hard, gem-like flame" of æsthetic observation, the flame of another altar mingled with the fire and darkened it. Not easily or surely shall we divine the workings of a brain and a conscience scarcely less complex, less fantastic, less enigmatical, than the face of Mona Lisa herself. Pater, as a human being, illustrated by no letters, by no diaries, by no impulsive unburdenings of himself to associates, will grow more and more shadowy. But it has seemed well to preserve, while still they are attainable, some of the external facts about a writer whose polished and concentrated work has already become part of the classic literature of England, and who will be remembered among the writers of this age when all but a few are forgotten.

September 1894

ROBERT LOUIS STEVENSON

Robert Louis Stevenson

PERSONAL MEMORIES

In setting down my recollections of Louis Stevenson, I desire to confine the record to what I have myself known and seen. His writings will be mentioned only in so far as I heard them planned and discussed. Of his career and character I shall not attempt to give a complete outline; all I purpose to do is to present those sides of them which came under my personal notice. The larger portrait it will be his privilege to prepare who was the closest and the most responsible of all Stevenson's friends; and it is only while we wait for Mr. Sidney Colvin's biography that these imperfect sketches can retain their value. The most that can be hoped for them is that they may secure a niche in his gallery. And now, pen in hand, I pause to think how I can render in words a faint impression of the most inspiriting, the most fascinating human being that I have known.

I

It is nearly a quarter of a century since I first saw Stevenson. In the autumn of 1870, in company with a former schoolfellow, I was in the Hebrides. We had been wandering in the Long Island, as they name the outer archipelago, and our steamer, returning, called at Skye. At the pier of Portree, I think, a company came on board—" people of importance in their day," Edinburgh acquaintances, I suppose, who had accidentally met in Skye on various errands. At all events, they invaded our modest vessel with a loud sound of talk. Professor Blackie was among them, a famous figure that calls for no description; and a voluble, shaggy man, clad in homespun, with spectacles forward upon nose, who, it was whispered to us, was Mr. Sam Bough, the Scottish Academician, a water-colour painter of some repute, who was to die in 1878. There were also several engineers of prominence. At the tail of this chatty, jesting little crowd of invaders came a youth of about my own age, whose appearance, for some mysterious reason, instantly attracted me. He was tall, preternaturally lean, with longish hair, and as restless and questing as a spaniel. The party from Portree fairly took possession of us; at meals they crowded around the captain, and we common tourists sat silent, below the salt. The stories of Blackie and Sam Bough were resonant. Meanwhile, I knew not why, I watched the plain, pale lad who took the lowest place in this privileged company.

The summer of 1870 remains in the memory of western Scotland as one of incomparable splendour. Our voyage, especially as evening drew on, was like an emperor's progress. We stayed on deck till the latest moment possible, and I occasionally watched the lean youth, busy and serviceable, with some of the little tricks with which we were later on to grow familiar— the advance with hand on hip, the sidewise bending of the head to listen. Meanwhile darkness overtook us, a wonderful halo of moonlight swam up over Glenelg, the indigo of the peaks of the Cuchullins faded into the general blue night. I went below, but was presently aware of some change of course, and then of an unexpected stoppage. I tore on deck, and found that we had left our track among the islands, and had steamed up a narrow and unvisited fiord of the mainland—I think Loch Nevis. The sight was curious and bewildering. We lay in a gorge of blackness, with only a strip of the blue moonlit sky overhead; in the dark a few lanterns jumped about the shore, carried by agitated but unseen and soundless persons. As I leaned over the bulwarks, Stevenson was at my side, and he explained to me that we had come up this loch to take away to Glasgow a large party of emigrants driven from their homes in the interests of a deer-forest. As he spoke, a black mass became visible entering the vessel. Then, as we slipped off shore, the fact of their hopeless exile came home to these poor fugitives, and suddenly, through the absolute silence, there rose from them a wild kerning and wailing, reverberated by the cliffs of the loch, and at that strange place and hour infinitely poignant. When I came on deck next morning, my unnamed friend was gone. He had put off with the engineers to visit some remote lighthouse of the Hebrides.

This early glimpse of Stevenson is a delightful memory to me. When we met next, not only did I instantly recall him, but, what was stranger, he remembered me. This voyage in the *Clansman* was often mentioned between us, and it has received for me a sort of consecration from the fact that in the very last letter that Louis wrote, finished on the day of his death, he made a reference to it.

II

In the very touching "Recollections" which our friend Mr. Andrew Lang has published, he says: "I shall not deny that my first impression [of Stevenson] was not wholly favourable." I remember, too, that John Addington Symonds was not pleased at first. It only shows how different are our moods. I must confess that in my case the invading army simply walked up and took the fort by storm. It was in 1877, or late in 1876, that I was presented to Stevenson, at the old Savile Club, by Mr. Sidney Colvin, who thereupon left us to our devices. We went downstairs and lunched together, and then we adjourned to the smoking-room. As twilight came on I tore myself away, but Stevenson walked with me across Hyde Park, and nearly to my house. He had an engagement, and so had I, but I walked a mile or two back with him. The fountains of talk had been unsealed, and they drowned the conventions. I came home dazzled with my new friend, saying, as Constance does of Arthur, "Was ever such a gracious creature born?" That impression of ineffable mental charm was formed at the first moment of acquaintance, and it never lessened or became modified. Stevenson's rapidity in the sympathetic interchange of ideas was, doubtless, the source of it. He has been described as an "egotist," but I challenge the description. If ever there was an altruist, it was Louis Stevenson; he seemed to feign an interest in himself merely to stimulate you to be liberal in your confidences.*

Those who have written about him from later impressions than those of which I speak seem to me to give insufficient prominence to the gaiety of Stevenson. It was his cardinal quality in those early days. A childlike mirth leaped and danced in him; he seemed to skip upon the hills of life. He was simply bubbling with quips and jests; his inherent earnestness or passion about abstract things was incessantly relieved by jocosity; and when he had built one of his intellectual castles in the sand, a wave of humour was certain to sweep in and destroy it. I cannot, for the life of me, recall any of his jokes; and written down in cold blood, they might not be funny if I did. They were not wit so much as humanity, the many-sided outlook upon

---

* This continued to be his characteristic to the last. Thus he described an interview he had in Sydney with some man formerly connected with the "black-birding" trade, by saying: "He was very shy at first, and it was not till I told him of a good many of my escapades that I could get him to thaw, and then he poured it all out. I have always found that the best way of getting people to be confidential."

life. I am anxious that his laughter-loving mood should not be forgotten, because later on it was partly, but I think never wholly, quenched by ill health, responsibility, and the advance of years. He was often, in the old days, excessively and delightfully silly—silly with the silliness of an inspired schoolboy; and I am afraid that our laughter sometimes sounded ill in the ears of age.

A pathos was given to his gaiety by the fragility of his health. He was never well, all the years I knew him; and we looked upon his life as hanging by the frailest tenure. As he never complained or maundered, this, no doubt—though we were not aware of it—added to the charm of his presence. He was so bright and keen and witty, and any week he might die. No one, certainly, conceived it possible that he could reach his forty-fifth year. In 1879 his health visibly began to run lower, and he used to bury himself in lonely Scotch and French places, "tinkering himself with solitude," as he used to say.

My experience of Stevenson during these first years was confined to London, upon which he would make sudden piratical descents, staying a few days or weeks, and melting into air again. He was much at my house; and it must be told that my wife and I, as young married people, had possessed ourselves of a house too large for our slender means immediately to furnish. The one person who thoroughly approved of our great, bare, absurd drawing-room was Louis, who very earnestly dealt with us on the immorality of chairs and tables, and desired us to sit always, as he delighted to sit, upon hassocks on the floor. Nevertheless, as arm-chairs and settees straggled into existence, he handsomely consented to use them, although never in the usual way, but with his legs thrown sidewise over the arms of them, or the head of a sofa treated as a perch. In particular, a certain shelf, with cupboards below, attached to a bookcase, is worn with the person of Stevenson, who would spend half an evening while passionately discussing some great question of morality or literature, leaping sidewise in a seated posture to the length of this shelf, and then back again. He was eminently peripatetic, too, and never better company than walking in the street, this exercise seeming to inflame his fancy. But his most habitual dwelling-place in the London of those days was the Savile Club, then lodged in an inconvenient but very friendly house in Savile Row. Louis pervaded the club; he was its most affable and chatty member; and he lifted it, by the ingenuity of his incessant dialectic, to the level of a sort of humorous Academe or Mouseion.

At this time he must not be thought of as a successful author. A very few of us were convinced of his genius; but with the exception of Mr. Leslie Stephen, nobody of editorial status was sure of it. I remember the publication of *An Inland Voyage* in 1878, and the inability of the critics and the public to see anything unusual in it.

Stevenson was not without a good deal of innocent oddity in his dress. When I try to conjure up his figure, I can see only a slight, lean lad, in a suit of blue sea-cloth, a black shirt, and a wisp of yellow carpet that did duty for a necktie. This was long his attire, persevered in to the anguish of his more conventional acquaintances. I have a ludicrous memory of going, in 1878, to buy him a new hat, in company with Mr. Lang, the thing then upon his head having lost the semblance of a human article of dress. Aided by a very civil shopman, we suggested several hats and caps, and Louis at first seemed interested; but having presently hit upon one which appeared to us pleasing and decorous, we turned for a moment to inquire the price. We turned back, and found that Louis had fled, the idea of parting with the shapeless object having proved too painful to be entertained. By the way, Mr. Lang will pardon me if I tell, in exacter detail, a story of his. It was immediately after the adventure with the hat that, not having quite enough money to take him from London to Edinburgh, third class, he proposed to the railway clerk to throw in a copy of Mr. Swinburne's *Queen-Mother and Rosamond*. The offer was refused with scorn, although the book was of the first edition, and even then worth more than the cost of a whole ticket.

Stevenson's pity was a very marked quality, and it extended to beggars, which is, I think, to go too far. His optimism, however, suffered a rude shock in South Audley Street one summer afternoon. We met a stalwart beggar, whom I refused to aid. Louis, however, wavered, and finally handed him sixpence. The man pocketed the coin, forbore to thank his benefactor, but, fixing his eye on me, said, in a loud voice, "And what is the other little gentleman going to give me?" "In future," said Louis, as we strode coldly on, "*I* shall be 'the other little gentleman.'"

In those early days he suffered many indignities on account of his extreme youthfulness of appearance and absence of self-assertion. He was at Inverness—being five or six and twenty at the time—and had taken a room in a hotel. Coming back about dinner-time, he asked the hour of table d'hôte, whereupon the landlady said, in a motherly way: "Oh, I knew you wouldn't like to sit in there among the grown-up people, so I've had a place put for you in the bar." There was a frolic at the Royal Hotel, Bathgate, in the summer of 1879. Louis was lunching alone, and the maid, considering him a negligible quantity, came and leaned out of the window. This outrage on the proprieties was so stinging that Louis at length made free to ask her, with irony, what she was doing there. "I'm looking for my lad," she replied. "Is that he?" asked Stevenson, with keener sarcasm. "Weel, I've been lookin' for him a' my life, and I've never seen him yet," was the response. Louis was disarmed at once, and wrote her on the spot some beautiful verses in the vernacular. "They're no bad for a beginner," she was kind enough to say when she had read them.

The year 1879 was a dark one in the life of Louis. He had formed a conviction that it was his duty to go out to the extreme west of the United States, while his family and the inner circle of his friends were equally certain that it was neither needful nor expedient that he should make this journey. As it turned out, they were wrong, and he was right; but in the circumstances their opinion seemed the only correct one. His health was particularly bad, and he was ordered, not West, but South. The expedition, which he has partly described in *The Amateur Emigrant* and *Across the Plains*, was taken, therefore, in violent opposition to all those whom he left in England and Scotland; and this accounts for the mode in which it was taken. He did not choose to ask for money to be spent in going to California, and it was hoped that the withdrawal of supplies would make the voyage impossible. But Louis, bringing to the front a streak of iron obstinacy which lay hidden somewhere in his gentle nature, scraped together enough to secure him a steerage passage across the Atlantic.

The day before he started he spent with my wife and me—a day of stormy agitation, an April day of rain-clouds and sunshine; for it was not in Louis to remain long in any mood. I seem to see him now, pacing the room, a cigarette spinning in his wasted fingers. To the last we were trying to dissuade him from what seemed to us the maddest of enterprises. He was so ill that I did not like to leave him, and at night—it was midsummer weather—we walked down into town together. We were by this time, I suppose, in a pretty hysterical state of mind, and as we went through Berkeley Square, in mournful discussion of the future, Louis suddenly proposed that we should visit the so-called " Haunted

House," which then occupied the newspapers. The square was quiet in the decency of a Sunday evening. We found the house, and one of us boldly knocked at the door. There was no answer and no sound, and we jeered upon the door-step; but suddenly we were both aware of a pale face—a phantasm in the dusk—gazing down upon us from a surprising height. It was the caretaker, I suppose, mounted upon a flight of steps: but terror gripped us at the heart, and we fled with foot-steps as precipitate as those of schoolboys caught in an orchard. I think that ghostly face in Berkeley Square must have been Louis's latest European impression for many months.

III

All the world now knows, through the two books which I have named, what immediately happened. Presently letters began to arrive, and in one from Monterey, written early in October 1879, he told me of what was probably the nearest approach of death that ever came until the end, fifteen years later. I do not think it is generally known, even in the inner circle of his friends, that in September of that year he was violently ill, alone, at an Angora-goat ranch in the Santa Lucia Mountains. "I scarcely slept or ate or thought for four days," he said. "Two nights I lay out under a tree, in a sort of stupor, doing nothing but fetch water for myself and horse, light a fire and make coffee, and all night awake hearing the goat-bells ringing and the tree-toads singing, when each new noise was enough to set me mad." Then an old frontiersman, a mighty hunter of bears, came round, and tenderly nursed him through his attack. "By all rule this should have been my death; but after a while my spirit got up again in a divine frenzy, and has since kicked and spurred my vile body forward with great emphasis and success."

Late in the winter of 1879, with renewed happiness and calm of life, and also under the spur of a need of money, he wrote with much assiduity. Among other things, he composed at Monterey the earliest of his novels, a book called *A Vendetta in the West*, the manuscript of which seems to have disappeared. Perhaps we need not regret it; for, so he declared to me, "It was about as bad as Ouida, but not quite, for it was not so eloquent." He had made a great mystery of his whereabouts; indeed, for several months no one was to know what had become of him, and his letters were to be considered secret. At length, in writing from Monterey, on November 15, 1879, he removed the embargo: "That I am in California may now be published to the brethren." In the summer of the next year, after a winter of very serious ill health, during which more than once he seemed on the brink of a galloping consumption, he returned to England. He had married in California a charming lady whom we all soon learned to regard as the most appropriate and helpful companion that Louis could possibly have secured. On October 8, 1880—a memorable day—he made his first appearance in London since his American exile. A post-card from

Edinburgh had summoned me to "appoint with an appointment" certain particular friends; "and let us once again," Louis wrote, "lunch together in the Savile Halls." Mr. Lang and Mr. Walter Pollock, and, I think, Mr. Henley, graced the occasion, and the club cellar produced a bottle of Chambertin of quite uncommon merit. Louis, I may explain, had a peculiar passion for Burgundy, which he esteemed the wine of highest possibilities in the whole Bacchic order; and I have often known him descant on a Pommard or a Montrachet in terms so exquisite that the listeners could scarcely taste the wine itself.

Davos-Platz was now prescribed for the rickety lungs; and late in that year Louis and his wife took up their abode there, at the Hôtel Buol, he carrying with him a note from me recommending him to the care of John Addington Symonds. Not at first, but presently and on the whole, these two men, so singular in their generation, so unique and so unlike, "hit it off," as people say, and were an intellectual solace to each other; but their real friendship did not begin till a later year. I remember Stevenson saying to me next spring that to be much with Symonds was to "adventure in a thornwood." It was at Davos, this winter of 1880, that Stevenson took up the study of Hazlitt, having found a publisher who was willing to bring out a critical and biographical memoir. This scheme occupied a great part of Louis's attention, but was eventually dropped; for the further he progressed in the investigation of Hazlitt's character the less he liked it, and the squalid

Liber Amoris gave the *coup de grâce*. He did not know what he would be at. His vocation was not yet apparent to him. He talked of writing on craniology and the botany of the Alps. The unwritten books of Stevenson will one day attract the scholiast, who will endeavour, perhaps, to reconstruct them from the references to them in his correspondence. It may, therefore, be permissible to record here that he was long proposing to write a life of the Duke of Wellington, for which he made some considerable collections. This was even advertised as "in preparation," on several occasions, from 1885 until 1887, but was ultimately abandoned. I remember his telling me that he intended to give emphasis to the "humour" of Wellington.

In June, 1881, we saw him again; but he passed very rapidly through London to a cottage at Pitlochry in Perthshire. He had lost his hold on town. "London," he wrote me, "now chiefly means to me Colvin and Henley, Leslie Stephen and you." He was now coursing a fresh literary hare, and set Mr. Austin Dobson, Mr. Saintsbury, and me busily hunting out facts about Jean Cavalier, the romantic eighteenth-century adventurer, whose life he fancied that he would write. His thoughts had recurred, in fact, to Scottish history; and he suddenly determined to do what seemed rather a mad thing—namely, to stand for the Edinburgh professorship of history, then just vacant. We were all whipped up for testimonials, and a little pamphlet exists, in a pearl-grey cover—the despair of bibliophiles—in which he and a strange assortment of his friends set forth his claims. These required nimble treatment, since, to put it plainly, it was impossible to say that he had any. His appeal was treated by the advocates, who were the electing body, with scant consideration, and some worthy gentleman was elected. The round Louis was well out of such a square hole as a chair in a university.

But something better was at hand. It was now, and in the peace of the Highlands, that Louis set out to become a popular writer. The fine art of "booming" had not then been introduced, nor the race of those who week by week discover coveys of fresh geniuses. Although Stevenson, in a sporadic way, had written much that was delightful, and that will last, he was yet —now at the close of his thirty-first year—by no means successful. The income he made by his pen was still ridiculously small; and Mr. John Morley, amazing as it sounds to-day, had just refused to give him a book to write in the *English Men of Letters* series, on the ground of his obscurity as an author. All this was to be changed, and the book that was to do it was even now upon the stocks. In August the Stevensons moved to a house in Braemar—a place, as Louis said, "patronised by the royalty of the Sister Kingdoms—Victoria and the Cairngorms, sir, honouring that country-side by their conjunct presence." Hither I was invited, and here I paid an ever memorable visit. The house, as Louis was careful to instruct me, was entitled "The Cottage, late the late Miss McGregor's, Castleton of Braemar"; and thus I obediently addressed my

T

letters until Louis remarked that "the reference to a deceased Highland lady, tending as it does to foster unavailing sorrow, may be with advantage omitted from the address."

To the Cottage, therefore, heedless of the manes of the late Miss McGregor, I proceeded in the most violent storm of hail and rain that even Aberdeenshire can produce in August, and found Louis as frail as a ghost, indeed, but better than I expected. He had adopted a trick of stretching his thin limbs over the back of a wicker sofa, which gave him an extraordinary resemblance to that quaint insect, the praying mantis; but it was a mercy to find him out of bed at all. Among the many attractions of the Cottage, the presence of Mr. Thomas Stevenson—Louis's father—must not be omitted. He was then a singularly charming and vigorous personality, indignantly hovering at the borders of old age ("Sixty-three, sir, this year; and, deuce take it! am I to be called 'an old gentleman' by a cab-driver in the streets of Aberdeen?") and, to my gratitude and delight, my companion in long morning walks. The detestable weather presently brought all the other members of the household to their beds, and Louis in particular became a wreck. However, it was a wreck that floated every day at nightfall; for at the worst he was able to come down-stairs to dinner and spend the evening with us.

We passed the days with regularity. After breakfast I went to Louis's bedroom, where he sat up in bed, with dark, flashing eyes and ruffled hair, and we played chess on the coverlet. Not a word passed, for he was strictly forbidden to speak in the early part of the day. As soon as he felt tired—often in the middle of a game—he would rap with peremptory knuckles on the board as a signal to stop, and then Mrs. Stevenson or I would arrange his writing materials on the bed. Then I would see no more of him till dinner-time, when he would appear, smiling and voluble, the horrid bar of speechlessness having been let down. Then every night, after dinner, he would read us what he had written during the day. I find in a note to my wife, dated September 3, 1881: "Louis has been writing, all the time I have been here, a novel of pirates and hidden treasure, in the highest degree exciting. He reads it to us every night, chapter by chapter." This, of course, was *Treasure Island*, about the composition of which, long afterward, in Samoa, he wrote an account in some parts of which I think that his memory played him false. I look back to no keener intellectual pleasure than those cold nights at Braemar, with the sleet howling outside, and Louis reading his budding romance by the lamplight, emphasising the purpler passages with lifted voice and gesticulating finger.

IV

Hardly had I left the Cottage than the harsh and damp climate of Aberdeenshire was felt to be rapidly destroying Louis, and he and his wife fled for Davos. Before the end of October they were ensconced there in a fairly comfortable châlet. Here Louis and his stepson amused themselves by setting up a hand-press, which Mr. Osbourne worked, and for which Louis provided the literary material. Four or five laborious little publications were put forth, some of them illustrated by the daring hand of Stevenson himself. He complained to me that Mr. Osbourne was a very ungenerous publisher—"one penny a cut, and one halfpenny a set of verses! What do you say to that for Grub Street?" These little diversions were brought to a close by the printer-publisher breaking, at one fell swoop, the press and his own finger. The little "Davos Press" issues now fetch extravagant prices, which would have filled author and printer with amazement. About this time Louis and I had a good deal of correspondence about a work which he had proposed that we should undertake in collaboration—a retelling, in choice literary form, of the most picturesque murder cases of the last hundred years. We were to visit the scenes of these crimes, and turn over the evidence. The great thing, Louis said, was not to begin to write until we were thoroughly alarmed. "These things must be done, my boy, under the very shudder of the goose-flesh." We were to begin with the "Story of the Red Barn," which indeed is a tale pre-eminently worthy to be retold by Stevenson. But the scheme never came off, and is another of the dead leaves in his Vallombrosa.

We saw him in London again, for a few days, in October 1882; but this was a melancholy period. For eight months at the close of that year and the beginning of 1883 he was capable of no mental exertion. He was in the depths of languor, and in nightly apprehension of a fresh attack. He slept excessively, and gave humorous accounts of the drowsiness that hung upon him, addressing his notes as "from the Arms of Porpus" (Morpheus) and "at the Sign of the Poppy." No climate seemed to relieve him, and so, in the autumn of 1882, a bold experiment was tried. As the snows of Davos were of no avail, the hot, damp airs of Hyères should be essayed. I am inclined to dwell in some fulness on the year he spent at Hyères, because, curiously enough, it was not so much as mentioned, to my knowledge, by any of the writers of obituary notices at Stevenson's death. It takes, nevertheless, a prominent place in his life's history, for his removal thither marked a sudden and brilliant, though only temporary, revival in his health and spirits. Some of his best work, too, was written at Hyères, and one might say that fame first found him in this warm corner of southern France.

The house at Hyères was called "La Solitude." It stood in a paradise of roses and aloes, fig-marigolds and olives. It had delectable and even, so Louis declared, "sub-celestial" views over a plain bounded by "certain mountains as graceful as Apollo, as severe as Zeus"; and at first the hot mistral, which blew and burned where it blew, seemed the only drawback. Not a few of the best poems in the *Underwoods* reflect the ecstasy of convalescence under the skies and perfumes of La Solitude. By the summer Louis could report "good health of a radiant order." It was while he was at Hyères that Stevenson first directly addressed an American audience, and I may record that, in September 1883, he told me to "beg Gilder your prettiest for a gentleman in pecuniary sloughs." Mr. Gilder was quite alive to the importance of securing such a contributor, although when the Amateur Emigrant had entered the office of *The Century Magazine* in 1879 he had been very civilly but coldly shown the door. (I must be allowed to tease my good friends in Union Square by recording that fact!) Mr. Gilder asked for fiction, but received instead *The Silverado Squatters*, which duly appeared in the magazine.

It was also arranged that Stevenson should make an ascent of the Rhône for *The Century*, and Mr. Joseph Pennell was to accompany him to make sketches for the magazine. But Stevenson's health failed again: the sudden death of a very dear old friend was a painful shock to him, and the winter of that year was not propitious. Abruptly, however, in January 1884, another crisis came. He went to Nice, where he was thought to be dying. He saw no letters; all his business was kindly taken charge of by Mr. Henley; and again, for a long time, he passed beneath the penumbra of steady languor and infirmity. When it is known how constantly he suffered, how brief and flickering were the intervals of comparative health, it cannot but add to the impression of his radiant fortitude through all these trials, and of his persistent employment of all his lucid moments. It was pitiful, and yet at the same time very inspiriting, to see a creature so feeble and so ill

equipped for the struggle bear himself so smilingly and
so manfully through all his afflictions. There can be
no doubt, however, that this latest breakdown vitally
affected his spirits. He was never, after this, quite
the gay child of genius that he had previously been.
Something of a graver cast became natural to his
thoughts; he had seen Death in the cave. And now
for the first time we traced a new note in his writings
—the note of " Pulvis et Umbra."

After 1883 my personal memories of Stevenson become very casual. In November 1884, he was settled
at Bournemouth, in a villa called Bonaltie Towers, and
there he stayed until, in March 1885, he took a house
of his own, which, in pious memory of his grandfather,
he named Skerryvore. In the preceding winter, when
I was going to America to lecture, he was particularly
anxious that I should lay at the feet of Mr. Frank R.
Stockton his homage, couched in the following lines:

> *My Stockton if I failed to like,*
>   *It were a sheer depravity;*
> *For I went down with the " Thomas Hyke,"*
>   *And up with the " Negative Gravity."*

He adored these tales of Mr. Stockton's, a taste which
must be shared by all good men. To my constant
sorrow, I was never able to go to Bournemouth during
the years he lived there. It has been described to me,
by those who were more fortunate, as a pleasure that
was apt to tantalize and evade the visitor, so constantly

was the invalid unable, at the last, to see the friend who had travelled a hundred miles to speak with him. It was therefore during his visits to London, infrequent as these were, that we saw him at his best, for these were made at moments of unusual recovery. He generally lodged at what he called the "Monument," this being his title for Mr. Colvin's house, a wing of the vast structure of the British Museum. I recall an occasion on which Louis dined with us (March 1886), because of the startling interest in the art of strategy which he had developed—an interest which delayed the meal with arrangements of serried bottles counterscarped and lines of cruets drawn up on horseback ready to charge. So infectious was his enthusiasm that we forgot our hunger, and hung over the embattled table-cloth, easily persuaded to agree with him that neither poetry nor the plastic arts could compete for a moment with "the finished conduct, sir, of a large body of men in face of the enemy."

It was a little later that he took up the practice of modelling clay figures as he sat up in bed. Some of these compositions—which needed, perhaps, his eloquent commentary to convey their full effect to the spectator—were not without a measure of skill of design. I recollect his saying, with extreme gravity, "I am in sculpture what Mr. Watts is in painting. We are both of us pre-occupied with moral and abstract ideas." I wonder whether any one has preserved specimens of these allegorical groups of clay.

The last time I had the happiness of seeing Stevenson was on Sunday, August 21, 1887. He had been brought up from Bournemouth the day before in a wretched condition of health, and was lodged in a private hotel in Finsbury Circus, in the City, ready to be easily moved to a steamer in the Thames on the morrow. I was warned, in a note, of his passage through town, and of the uncertainty whether he could be seen. On the chance, I went over early on the 21st, and, very happily for me, he had had a fair night, and could see me for an hour or two. No one else but Mrs. Stevenson was with him. His position was one which might have daunted any man's spirit, doomed to exile, in miserable health, starting vaguely across the Atlantic, with all his domestic interests rooted up, and with no notion where, or if at all, they should be replanted. If ever a man of imagination could be excused for repining, it was now.

But Louis showed no white feather. He was radiantly humorous and romantic. It was church time, and there was some talk of my witnessing his will, which I could not do, because there could be found no other reputable witness, the whole crew of the hotel being at church. This set Louis off on a splendid dream of romance. "This," he said, "is the way in which our valuable city hotels—packed, doubtless, with rich objects of jewellery—are deserted on a Sunday morning. Some bold piratical fellow, defying the spirit of Sabbatarianism, might make a handsome revenue by sacking the derelict hotels between the hours of ten and twelve. One hotel a week would suffice to enable such

a man to retire into private life within the space of a
year. A mask might, perhaps, be worn for the mere
fancy of the thing, and to terrify kitchen-maids, but
no real disguise would be needful to an enterprise
that would require nothing but a brave heart and a
careful study of the City Postal Directory." He
spoke of the matter with so much fire and gallantry
that I blushed for the youth of England and its lack
of manly enterprise. No one ever could describe
preposterous conduct with such a convincing air as
Louis could. Common sense was positively humbled
in his presence.

The volume of his poems called *Underwoods* had just
appeared, and he inscribed a copy of it to me in the
words "at Todgers', as ever was, *chez Todgers*, Peck-
sniff street." The only new book he seemed to wish
to carry away with him was Mr. Hardy's beautiful
romance, *The Woodlanders*, which we had to scour
London that Sunday afternoon to get hold of. In the
evening Mr. Colvin and I each returned to "Todgers'"
with the three volumes, borrowed or stolen somewhere,
and wrapped up for the voyage next day. And so the
following morning, in an extraordinary vessel called the
Ludgate Hill—as though in compliment to Mr. Stockton's genius—and carrying, besides the Stevensons,
a cargo of stallions and monkeys, Mr. and Mrs. Stevenson and Mr. Lloyd Osbourne steamed down the Thames
in search of health across the Atlantic and the Pacific.
The horses, Louis declared, protruded their noses in an
unmannerly way between the passengers at dinner,

and the poor little grey monkeys, giving up life for a
bad job on board that strange, heaving cage, died by
dozens, and were flung contemptuously out into the
ocean. The strangest voyage, however, some time
comes to an end, and Louis landed in America. He
was never to cross the Atlantic again; and for those
who loved him in Europe he had already journeyed
more than half-way to another world.

V

It is impossible to deal, however lightly, with the
personal qualities of Robert Louis Stevenson without
dwelling on the extreme beauty of his character. In
looking back over the twenty years in which I knew
him, I feel that, since he was eminently human, I ought
to recall his faults, but I protest that I can remember
none. Perhaps the nearest approach to a fault was a
certain want of discretion, always founded on a wish to
make people understand each other, but not exactly
according to wisdom. I recollect that he once em-
broiled me for a moment with John Addington Symonds
in a manner altogether bloodthirsty and ridiculous, so
that we both fell upon him and rended him. This
little weakness is really the blackest crime I can lay to
his charge. And on the other side, what courage, what
love, what an indomitable spirit, what a melting pity!
He had none of the sordid errors of the little man
who writes—no sick ambition, no envy of others, no
exaggeration of the value of this ephemeral trick of

scribbling. He was eager to help his fellows, ready to take a second place, with great difficulty offended, by the least show of repentance perfectly appeased.

Quite early in his career he adjusted himself to the inevitable sense of physical failure. He threw away from him all the useless impediments: he sat loosely in the saddle of life. Many men who get such a warning as he got take up something to lean against; according to their education or temperament, they support their maimed existence on religion, or on cynical indifference, or on some mania of the collector or the *dilettante*. Stevenson did none of these things. He determined to make the sanest and most genial use of so much of life as was left him. As any one who reads his books can see, he had a deep strain of natural religion; but he kept it to himself; he made no hysterical or ostentatious use of it.

Looking back at the past, one recalls a trait that had its significance, though one missed its meaning then. He was careful, as I have hardly known any other man to be, not to allow himself to be burdened by the weight of material things. It was quite a jest with us that he never acquired any possessions. In the midst of those who produced books, pictures, prints, bric-à-brac, none of these things ever stuck to Stevenson. There are some deep-sea creatures, the early part of whose life is spent dancing through the waters; at length some sucker or tentacle touches a rock, adheres, pulls down more tentacles, until the creature is caught there, stationary for the remainder of its existence.

So it happens to men, and Stevenson's friends, one after another, caught the ground with a house, a fixed employment, a "stake in life;" he alone kept dancing in the free element, unattached. I remember his saying to me that if ever he had a garden he should like it to be empty, just a space to walk and talk in, with no flowers to need a gardener nor fine lawns that had to be mown. Just a fragment of the bare world to move in, that was all Stevenson asked for. And we who gathered possessions around us—a little library of rare books, a little gallery of drawings or bronzes—he mocked us with his goblin laughter; it was only so much more luggage to carry on the march, he said, so much more to strain the arms and bend the back.

Stevenson thought, as we all must think, that literature is a delightful profession, a primrose path. I remember his once saying so to me, and then he turned, with the brimming look in his lustrous eyes and the tremulous smile on his lips, and added, "But it is not all primroses, some of it is brambly, and most of it uphill." He knew—no one better—how the hill catches the breath and how the brambles tear the face and hands; but he pushed strenuously, serenely on, searching for new paths, struggling to get up into the light and air.

One reason why it was difficult to be certain that Stevenson had reached his utmost in any direction was what I will call, for want of a better phrase, the *energetic modesty* of his nature. He was never satisfied with himself, yet never cast down. There are two dangers that beset the artist—the one is being pleased with what he has done, and the other being dejected with it. Stevenson, more than any other man whom I have known, steered the middle course. He never conceived that he had achieved a great success, but he never lost hope that by taking pains he might yet do so. Twelve years ago, when he was beginning to write that curious and fascinating book, *Prince Otto*, he wrote to me describing the mood in which one should go about one's work—golden words, which I have never forgotten. "One should strain," he said, "and then play, strain again, and play again. The strain is for us, it educates; the play is for the reader, and pleases. In moments of effort one learns to do the easy things that people like."

He learned that which he desired, and he gained more than he hoped for. He became the most exquisite English writer of his generation; yet those who lived close to him are apt to think less of this than of the fact that he was the most unselfish and the most lovable of human beings.

1895.

PRINTED AT
THE BALLANTYNE PRESS
LONDON

INDEX

Across the Plains, Stevenson's 284
Addison, Joseph, 71, 90
Æschylus, 39, 78, 81
Æschylus, trans. by Fitz-Gerald, 78, 81
Agamemnon, trans. by Fitz-Gerald, 78
Alastor, Shelley's 191
Alciati, 191
Alciphron, Berkeley's 74
Alfarabi, Beddoes' 34
Amateur Emigrant, Stevenson's *The*, 284
Amoretti, Spenser's 9
Andersen, Hans, 130
Anna Karenine, Tolstoi's 117, 125, 127, 130
Appreciations, with an Essay on Style, Pater's 259
Ariosto, Lodovico, 26
Arnold, Matthew, 145, 172, 178, 183
Asselineau, Charles, 221
Assja, Tourgenieff's 124
Atalanta in Calydon, Swinburne's 147, 174–175
Ayres for the Theorbo, Henry Lawes' 192

BADER, Clarisse, 205–207

Bailey, Philip James, 22, 145, 171
Barrett, Edward, 13
Barrett, Elizabeth, 1, 4, 6–10, 32, 145
Barton, Bernard, 66, 70–71, 73
Bathurst, Lady, 170
Beddoes, Dr. Thomas, 33
Beddoes, Thomas Lovell, 31–61
Bengal Magazine, 203, 209
Benson, Mr. Arthur Christopher, 194
Berkeley's *Alciphron*, 74
Bevan, C.D., 33
Biographische Aufsätze, 251
Bird Parliament, The, trans. by FitzGerald, 89–90
Blackie, Prof., 276
Blake, William, 191
Blessed Damozel, D. G. Rossetti's *The*, 144, 146
Blumenbach, Prof., 40, 42
Book-plates, A Guide to the Study of, De Tabley's 192
Borrow, George, 78
Bough, Sam, 276
Breughel, Helsche, 52
Bride's Tragedy, Beddoes' *The*, 34, 51, 56–57
Browne, Sir Thomas, 183

Index

Browning, Elizabeth Barrett, 1-17, 57, 136, 172
  Poems of, 1850 Edition, 1
  Sonnets from the Portuguese, 1-17
  The Seraphim, 4
Browning, Robert, 1-5, 13, 32, 55, 57-59, 145, 172, 183, 191
Browning, Robert Barrett, 61
Bussell, Rev. F. W., 260
Byron, 26, 31, 138
Bywater, Mr. Ingram, 248

Calcutta Review, The, 209
Calderon de la Barca, Pedro, *Six Dramas of*, trans. by FitzGerald, 75, 80-81
Campbell, J. Dykes, 56, 61
Campbell, Thomas, 32
Capes, Mr. W. W., 248, 250
Carlyle, Thomas, 66, 68, 70, 71, 72, 75
Catarina to Camoens, 3
Catullus, 230
Cavalier, Jean, 288
Chapman, George, 84
Chenier, André, 204
Child in the House, Pater's 259
Childhood, Boyhood, Youth, Tolstoi's 119
Clarke, Cowden, 22
Clinton, Lord Edward, 167
Clough, A. H., 145, 172
Coleridge, Samuel Taylor, 32, 250
Columbus, Admiral Diego, 218
Colvin, Sir Sidney, 275, 278, 288, 296
Congreve, William, 90
Conjugal Happiness, Tolstoi's 123

Coppée, François, 219
Cornwall, Barry, 35, 52
Cossacks, Tolstoi's *The*, 120-121
Cowell, E. B., 75-76, 78, 87
Cowper, Henry, 167
Cowper, William, 90, 160, 243
Crabbe, George, 66, 81
Crashaw, Richard, 156, 183
Creighton, Dr. Mandell, 252-253, 255, 270
Curzon, Robert, 167
Cynthia and Bugboo, Beddoes' 34

DANTE, 160
Darley, George, 31, 38
Daudet, Alphonse, 270
Davidson, John, 194
Davos Press, The, 292
Dead Souls, Gogol's 118
Death of Ivan Iliitch, Tolstoi's *The*, 128-129
Death's Jest-Book, Beddoes' 32, 39-43, 49, 51
Defence of Guinevere, FitzGerald's 82
Defence of Guinevere, Morris's 147
Degen the Baker, 46-49
de Lisle, Leconte, 203, 219, 227, 229
De Quincey's *Opium-Eater*, 71
Desbordes-Valmore, Marceline, 12, 206
de Tabley, Lord, 165-195
Dierx, Léon, 219
Digby, Sir Kenelm, 74, 75
Dilke, Charles Wentworth, 22
Dobson, Austin, 186, 193, 263, 288

Index

Donatello, 230
Donne, W. B., 67
Dostoieffsky, 118, 124
Dream Pedlary, Beddoes' 54
Dryden, John, 84–85, 89, 136
Duff, Sir Mountstuart Grant, 170, 189
Dutt, Govin Chunder, 201
Dutt, Toru, 199–212
Dyer, Sir W. T. Thiselton-, 189

Ecclesiastical Sonnets, Wordsworth's 10
Ecklin, Dr., 48–49, 59
Eclogues and Monodramas, De Tabley's 174
Edgeworth, Maria, 33
Emerson, R. W., 98
Endymion, Keats' 22
English Men of Letters Series, 289
Enoch Arden, Tennyson's 172
Erinna, 136–138
Euphranor, FitzGerald's 74, 91
Euripides, 39
Examiner, The, 199

FAIRFAX, Edward, 84
Festus, Bailey's 145
Fielding, Henry, 34
FitzGerald, Edward, 65–92, 153
Fletcher, Giles, 26, 184
Fortesque, George, 167–169
Fortnightly Review, The, 154, 175, 222, 242, 251, 258
Fragmenta Aurea, Suckling's 191
France, M. Anatole, 220

Franks, Sir A. W., 189
Frey, Dr., 44

GAUTIER, Théophile, 220
Germ, Rossetti's (C. G.) *The*, 144–146
Gladstone, W. E., 169, 177
Goblin Market, Christina Rossetti's 142, 147, 149–151
Goethe, 9, 250–251
Goldsmith, Oliver, 263
Gontcharoff, 118, 124
Grammont, Count de, 207
Gray, Thomas, 90, 188, 265
Green, T. H., 250

HALLAM, Arthur, 167
Haydon, Benjamin Robert, 22
Hegel, 251
Hegetschweiler, 43
Henley, William Ernest 287–288, 294
Herbert, George, 156
Heredia, A. don Pedro de, 218
Heredia, José-Maria de, 215–237
Herzlieb, Minna, 9
Hinchinbrooke, Lord, 168
Holstein, Prince Frederick of, 167
Holy Living and Holy Dying, Jeremy Taylor's 97
Homer, 26, 84, 137
Hood, Thomas, 32
Houghton, Lord, 25, 79, 169–170
House of Life, Rossetti's 9, 222
House of the Dead, Dostoieffsky's *The*, 124
Hunt, Leigh, 21

Index

Hyères, Stevenson at, 293, 294
Hyperion, Keats' 229

Idylls of the King, Tennyson's 172
Imaginary Portraits, Pater's 259
Improvisatore, Beddoes' *The*, 32, 34, 55–56
Inclusions, E. B. Browning's 16
Inland Voyage, Stevenson's 281
Ivory Gate, Beddoes' 43

JAHN, Otto, 251
Jami (Persian Poet), 76, 87–89
Jamieson, Mrs., 1
Johnson, Lionel, 242
Johnson, Dr. Samuel, 77
Jowett, Prof., 248–249

KEAN, Edmund, 33
Keats, George, 28
Keats, John, 5, 21–28, 31, 32, 37, 97, 144, 183, 224
Keble, John, 247
Kelsall, Thomas Forbes, 31, 35–41, 45, 49, 56–58, 60–61
Kemble, J. M., 67
King, Miss Emmeline, 49
King, Miss Zoë, 46–47, 49, 57–59
Kipling, Mr. Rudyard, 265
Kreutzner Sonata, Tolstoi's 122

LABÉ, Louise, 12
Lamartine, Alphonse de, 25
Lamb, Charles, 67, 69

"Lancaster, William," 172, 178–179
Landon, Letitia Elizabeth, 31
Landor, Walter Savage, 37, 53
Lang, Andrew, 278, 282, 287
Leaves of Grass, Walt Whitman's 98–99
Leighton, The Hon. Lady, 171
Lepage, Bastien, 129
Lermantof, 120
Lewes, G. H., 175
Liebig, Baron, 44
Livre de Sonnets, De Heredia's 221
Longley, Sir Henry, 167
Loti, M. Pierre, 119
Love's Arrow Poisoned, Beddoes' 36
Lucretius, 230

MACAULAY, Lord, 32
Macready, W. C., 33
Madagascar, Davenant's 191
Mallarmé, Stéphane, 219
Marius the Epicurean, Pater's 258–259, 262, 267
Marlowe, Christopher, 34, 38
Marston, John, 52
Martial, 230
Massinger, 38
Maud, Tennyson's 145
Mazade, M. de, 216
Men and Women, Robert Browning's 172
Mendès, Catulle, 219
Mexique, La Conquête du, trans. by De Heredia, 235
Middleton, Thomas, 36
Milnes, Monckton, *see* Houghton, Lord
Milton, John, 24, 26, 183, 190, 224

Minto, Prof. William, 199–200
Mirandola, Barry Cornwall's 35
Miscellaneous Studies, Pater's 245, 250
Mitford, Mary Russell, 3
Moore, Thomas, 32
Morley, Viscount, 289
Morning Post, The, 34
Morris, William, 147–148, 252, 261
Mort de Valmiki, De Lisle's 203
My Beautiful Lady, Woolner's 147

Nest of Nobles, Tourgenieff's 124
Newman, Cardinal, 75, 156
Newton, John, 160
Nikolaievitch, Lyof, *see* Tolstoi

Oblomof, Gontcharoft's 124
Omar Khayyám, FitzGerald's 65, 77–90
On Idlers and Idling, Stevenson's 141
Orestes, De Tabley's 177–179
Osbourne, Mr. Lloyd, 292, 298
Outidana, Beddoes' 39

Parnasse Contemporain, The, 219–221
Pater, Jean Baptiste, 242
Pater, Richard Glode, 243–244
Pater, Walter, 241–271
Pater, Wm. Thomson, 244
Patmore, Coventry, 145
Pattison, Mark, 255–256
Phillips, R., Letter from Beddoes to, 48

Philoctetes, De Tabley's 170 175–177
Pinero, Sir Arthur Wing, 267
Pisemsky, 118, 124
Plato and Platonism, Pater's 259, 264
Poems and Ballads, Swinburne's 153
Polidori, G. —, 138, 142
Polikouchka, Tolstoi's 121–122
Pollock, Sir Frederick, 75
Pollock, Mr. Walter, 287
Polonius, FitzGerald's 74
Pope, Alexander, 25, 84
Portuguese, Sonnets from the Browning's 1–17
Posthumous Poems, Shelley's 36
Pouchkine, 120
Praed, William Mackworth, 32
Praeterita, Lord de Tabley's 172
Price, Bonamy, 252–253
Prince Otto, Stevenson's 302
Prince's Progress, Christina Rossetti's 149–151
Procter, Bryan Waller, 35–37, 41–46, 58
Procter, Mrs., 37, 45
Prudhomme, Sully, 219, 225
Purcell, Edward, 66

Quarles, Francis, 191

Racine, Jean, 97, 179
Redcliffe, Lord Stratford de 168
Rehearsals, De Tabley's 179
Ronsard, Pierre de, 224
Rossetti, Christina, 135–162, 224, 261
    Personal Recollections of, 157–162

Index

Rossetti, Dante Gabriel, 10, 79, 82, 138–140, 144, 148, 154–155, 178, 219, 254, 261
Rossetti, Maria Francesca, 160
Rousseau's *Discours* of 1750, 108
Rubáiyát of Omar Khayyám, FitzGerald's 65, 77–90, 153
Ruskin, John, 79, 251

SAINTSBURY, Prof. George, 204, 288
Salámán and Absál, Fitz-Gerald's 76, 86–89
Sandwich, Lord, *see* Hinchinbrooke, 168
Sappho, 5, 136–138
Schiller, 39
Schoenlien (Surgeon), 42
Scott, Sir Walter, 32
Scott, William Bell, 254
Searching the Net, De Tabley's 179
Second Brother, Beddoes' 35, 38
Selden, John, 75
Shadwell, Mr. Charles Lancelot, 249
Shakespeare, 2, 6, 10, 13, 33, 69, 135, 153, 224
Sheaf gleaned in French Fields, Dutt's *A*, 200–212
Shelley, P. B., 22, 26, 31, 32, 35, 36, 53, 106, 152, 153
Silverado Squatters, Stevenson's *The*, 294
Six Dramas of Calderon, trans. by Edward FitzGerald, 75, 80, 81
Sketches from Sevastopol, Tolstoi's 123
Smith, Alexander, 204

Soldier of Fortune, De Tabley's *The*, 180
Sonnets from the Portuguese, E. B. Browning's 1–17
Sophocles, trans. by FitzGerald, 81
Soulary, Joséphin, 203
Southey, Robert, 32
Spectator, The, 170
Spedding, James, 66, 67, 74
Spenser, Edmund, 9, 10, 26, 192, 224
Stephen, Sir Leslie, 281, 288
Stevenson, Robert Louis, 98, 141, 265, 275–302
  Personal Memories of 275–302
Stevenson, Thomas, 290
Stockton, Frank R., 295, 298
Story of a Horse, Tolstoi's *The*, 130
Strayed Reveller, Arnold's 145
Studies in the History of the Renaissance, Pater's 252
Studies in Verse, De Tabley's 174
Swinburne, Algernon Charles, 79, 85, 97, 147, 148, 153, 161, 174, 254, 261, 282
Swinton, J. R., 168
Symonds, John Addington, 98, 278, 287, 299

TACITUS, 71
Tale of a Tub, Swift's *The*, 72
Talfourd, Thomas Noon, 52
Tassy, Garcin de, 77, 205
Taylor, Jeremy, 71, 97, 183
Taylor, William, 37
Tennyson, Lord, 4–5, 24, 25, 32, 65, 67, 69, 71–73, 77, 85, 91, 106, 144–145, 152, 165, 167, 170, 172, 177, 184

Index

Thackeray, W. M., 66–69, 73
Theuriet, André, 199
Thompson (of Trinity), W. H., 66–67
Thoreau, H. D., 98
Thousand Souls, Pisemsky's *A*, 124
Three Deaths, Tolstoi's 124–125
Tiresias, Tennyson's 65
Tolstoi, Count Lyof, 115–131
Torrismond, Beddoes' 35, 38, 53
Tourgenieff, 118, 124, 128
Tourneur, Cyril, 36, 52, 184
Treasure Island, R. L. Stevenson's 291
Trophées, De Heredia's *Les* 223, 225–228

Underwoods, Stevenson's 298
Undine, Fouqué's 69

VALMORE, Marceline, 12, 206
Vaughan, Henry, 156
Vendetta in the West, Stevenson's *A*, 286
Verlaine, Paul, 219
Verses by Christina G. Rossetti, 142
Virgil, 25, 230
Vishnupurana, The, 209
Vogüé, Vicomte de, 120

Wahlverwandtschaften, Goethe's 10
Walpole, Horace, 72
War and Peace, Tolstoi's 122, 125–127, 129
Ward, Humphry, Mrs., 255
Warren, John Byrne Leicester, 166–180
Watson, William, 194
Watts, George Frederick, 296
Watts-Dunton, Mr. Theodore, 159, 194
Webster, John, 36, 38
Wellington, Duke of, 288
White, Blanco, 210
Whitman, Walt, 95–111
Winchilsea, Lady, 12
Winckelmann, Life of, Otto Jahn, 251
    Pater's *Essay on*, 251
Wither, George, 156
Woodlanders, Mr. Thomas Hardy's 298
Woolner, Thomas, 147
Wordsworth, William, 4, 7–8, 10, 22, 32, 68–69, 145, 151, 173, 183, 222, 224
Wright, Mr. Aldis, 73, 79, 83, 90

ZOLA, 129, 215–216
Zouche, Lord, 166